Bob Harrison's On This Day

Fifty Great Days in History

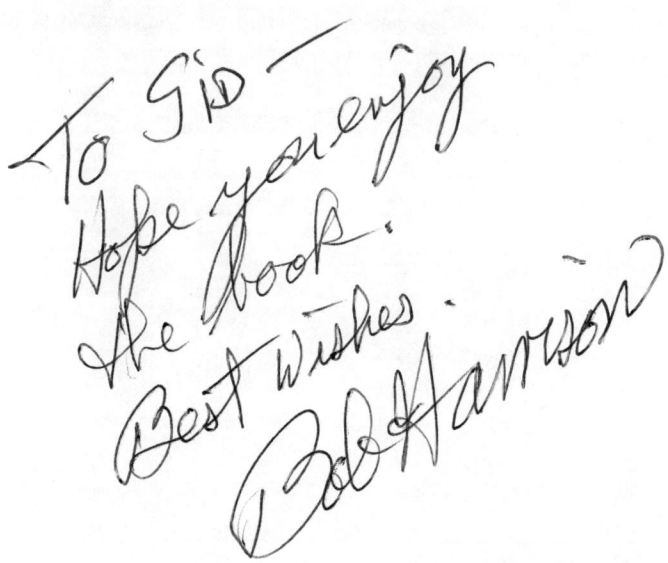

Library of Congress Control Number: 2011903513
ISBN: Hardcover   978-1-4568-8020-0
               Softcover   978-1-4568-8019-4
               Ebook   978-1-4568-8021-7

To order additional copies of this book, contact:
Xlibris Corporation
1-888-795-4274
www.Xlibris.com
Orders@Xlibris.com
91082

Contents

April

May

June

July

August

September

October

November

December

This book is lovingly dedicated to Miss Marion Diehl, my sixth-grade teacher, who first showed me the excitement of learning and the joys of knowing history.

Acknowledgments

I wrote the material in this book, but I never could have handled all of the intricacies of the publishing process.

Frank Stearn, Bill Pukmel, and Richard Michalski were of invaluable help in electronically gathering and organizing the original "On This Day" items.

Emily Harrison Weir and Susan Harrison Michalski were equally indispensible in helping me select among the candidates for publication, tracking down the appropriate graphics and permissions, editing as necessary, and pushing forward the publishing process to a successful conclusion.

I thank them all.

Foreword

This is a book about history.

I confess. I have always loved history. The affair began with a subscription to the *Weekly Reader* in third grade at Marion, Pennsylvania's two-room schoolhouse. Hitler was coming to power in Germany. The *Hindenburg* burned and crashed at Lakehurst, New Jersey, Naval Air Station. FDR was remaking the face of America. A civil war was raging in China. Well, you get the picture, I'm sure.

Next came the exciting events of the late '30s and the magnetic teaching of Miss Marion Diehl at Chambersburg's Buchanan Grade School. I suspect that we both admired the same muse, for Miss Diehl used the daily newspapers like textbooks. Radio helped a lot also. A new pope was raised, the Japanese sunk the USS *Panay* in the Yangtze River, and the German Rhineland was being remilitarized at the direction of the new German chancellor. The Lindbergh baby was kidnapped and murdered. The Dionne quintuplets were born. FDR came to Gettysburg for the seventy-fifth anniversary of the battle. History was so exciting. I could hardly wait to grow up to learn more firsthand by traveling.

In just a few short years, I got that opportunity—courtesy of the US Navy—and continued traveling later on my own with my history-loving, French-speaking, enthusiastically traveling wife, Françoise.

In short, history—properly presented—is addictive. During the past twenty-five years, I've hopefully been making the stories in this book compelling—first on daily "ON THIS DAY" broadcasts on the former WKSL Radio and later in my monthly ON THIS DAY columns in the *Public Opinion* newspaper.

You are holding the fruits of years of labor and a lifetime of love of the subject. *Enjoy*!—Bob Harrison

JANUARY

The *Challenger* explodes
Credit: NASA

Challenger Explosion:
Christa, We All Miss Ya

It was one of those days that you never forget where you were or what you were doing.

ON THIS DAY, January 28, 1986, I was in Nashville, Tennessee, not attending The Grand Ole Opry, but at the Opryland Hotel undergoing a rigorous week of training to become qualified to be a Rotary District Governor.

With me were nearly a thousand other trainees and their wives from 160 countries around the Rotary world. At that moment we were about as close as anyone could be to being a little United Nations, all packed into a giant auditorium and housed in a single building.

This was the day that the United States space program went up in smoke and crashed in flames!

It all happened in just seventy-three seconds, televised for the entire world to see. The space shuttle *Challenger* had blown up shortly after takeoff and crashed into the Atlantic Ocean just a few miles away from Cape Kennedy. All seven astronauts were dead before they hit the water!

When the disaster was announced to our Rotary group, everything stopped. An unearthly moan arose from the audience, followed by sobs and cries of "Oh, no!"

Immediately, many of those men and women rushed toward the Americans and wrapped us in their consoling physical and verbal embraces. It was one of those times when I truly felt that we were all dependent members of the same world.

Challenger was the second in a series of space shuttles designed to transport cargo into space and then to return to Earth for more flights. And *Challenger* had flawlessly done just that, flying nine successful missions from its first launch in 1981 until that fateful day just five years later.

True, *Challenger's* final launch was plagued by problems, mostly due to the windy, chilly weather. Launch dates were tried on January 22, 23, 24, 25, and 27, but had to be scrubbed each time. Finally, the spaceship was committed at 11:38 a.m. EST, On This Day, January 28, 1986.

The names of six of the seven astronauts on board are already fading into the obscurity of space exploration history, but that seventh crewmember's name still rolls readily off the tongue.

She was to have been the first teacher in space, chosen from an incredible list of 11,000 teacher volunteers who had applied! Her students were watching in their classroom and so were thousands of other students around the country and indeed all over the world. Everyone was full of enthusiasm and ready for liftoff.

It was not to be.

QUESTION: What was this adventurous teacher's never-to-be-forgotten name?

ANSWER: She was Christa McAuliffe, a New Hampshire schoolteacher, victim of bad luck, bad weather, and a bad "O" ring.

Gold Discovered in California

I sometimes think that we latecomers to American "civilization" have missed all the fun. For example, ON THIS DAY, January 24, 1848, one James Marshall, foreman of a sawmill building crew, seemed to be having a bit of trouble with a few hunks of metal fouling up the mill race of a newly built sawmill.

You probably can guess what happened next. "Big Jim" Marshall filled his pockets with several of the offending chunks of shiny metal and went running full-tilt to see the boss—John Sutter—yelling Gold! Gold! Gold!

Sutter, at whose mill the gold had been found, was not amused.

"For God's sake, man, keep your voice down. If word of this gets out we will be overrun by gold-seekers. My sawmill and farming business will be ruined!"

But, contrary to Sutter's orders, word got out almost immediately that gold had been discovered at the confluence of the Feather, Sacramento, and American Rivers in California's Sierra Nevada Mountains. Soon would-be miners from all over were chartering clipper ships in New York City for the arduous eight-month, 18,000-nautical-mile trip around the tip of South America!

In addition to Americans, thousands more came from Australia, New Zealand, France, Germany, Italy, Great Britain, China, Hawaii, Mexico, and various parts of South America. The nearest deep-water harbor to the gold fields was San Francisco, but soon that sheltered bay was filled with ships!

Anxious to get at the gold, their entire crews abandoned ship and swam ashore. After all, the gold fields were essentially public lands, free for the staking and the working. Within two years, San Francisco went from a population of 1,000 to more than 25,000 people! The area known as California in February of 1848 went from being part of the spoils of the Mexican War to become a somewhat lawless quasi-territory, to finally evolving into a full-fledged US state in 1850.

Eventually the "forty-niners," as they later came to be known, also came to California overland by wagon train from the eastern United States. Some even chose a different sailing route, using a land-portage across the Isthmus of Panama as a short cut.

It was a wild time to be sure, but by 1855 most of the excitement had died down.

QUESTION: How many newcomers would you say had descended upon California in those seven years?

ANSWER: It is estimated that more than 300,000 gold seekers, merchants, cardsharps, and ladies of easy virtue had arrived in the Golden State since that fateful day at Sutter's Mill. And it turned out that John Sutter was prescient. His lands and his businesses were stolen, overrun, and destroyed by gold seekers. He died penniless. We don't know what happened to "Big Jim" Marshall. Now aren't you sorry to have missed all of the fun?

Nelly Bly: "Pink" Makes it in Record Time

When she was born they called her "Pink," had her christened in a bright pink gown, and showered her with the fruits of middle-class Victorian life in America.

Elizabeth Jane Cochran was born at the close of the Civil War in the tiny western Pennsylvania village of Cochran's Mills, near Pittsburgh. Her father, a judge, was the leading citizen of the town. Life was wonderful, but soon it would change drastically for the worse.

When Pink was just six years old, her father died suddenly, without a will and having made no provision for his wife and family. Her mother had to sell the family home in order to settle the estate. Shortly after her husband's demise, the new widow became a new bride, hoping to insure security for her young family. Unfortunately, Pink, her siblings, and her mother were terribly abused by the new husband, leaving permanent scars on the impressionable youngsters.

As soon as she turned eighteen, Pink set out on her life's work, newspapering, something that no well-bred, self-respecting Victorian lady would do. She was a talented writer, and almost immediately was hired by the *Pittsburgh Dispatch*, given the new name "Nelly Bly" (after a popular Stephen Foster song of the day), and put to work at the new newspaper task of investigative reporting.

She focused on women's-rights issues, poverty, workers' rights, and political corruption. As a matter of fact, Nelly did her work *so* well that the paper's advertisers threatened to cancel their ads unless she stopped her "snooping." So, of course, she was promptly fired.

Undaunted, Nelly Bly high-tailed it to New York City and nearly starved to death for four months until she was able to talk her way into a job at the tabloid *New York World*. It was just not any job, mind you; she had talked them into sending her on a well-publicized race around the world, determined to best the record of the fictitious Phileas Fogg, the hero of Jules Verne's *Around the World in Eighty Days*!

On November 14, 1889, twenty-five-year-old Nelly Bly was off and running—east to west—on her maiden voyage. She made it home in record time!

QUESTION: How long do you think it took Nelly Bly to circumnavigate the globe?

ANSWER: In seventy-two days, six hours, eleven minutes, and fourteen seconds, Nelly Bly returned to Hoboken, New Jersey, from whence she had departed; and she did it ON THIS DAY, January 25, 1890.

Alice in Wonderland

ON THIS DAY, January 27, 1832, in Cheshire, England, Charles Lutwidge Dodgson was born! What, you say you've never heard of Charles Dodgson, the famous author, poet, mathematician, Anglican clergyman, Oxford don, professional photographer, and logician? Well, perhaps if I tell you he sometimes wrote under the pen name of Lewis Carroll and that he was most famous for authoring *Alice's Adventures in Wonderland*, the "Aha!" light above your head will come on. There, I thought so.

Carroll, as we shall now call him, was born some five years before the Victorian Age began in Merrie Olde England, and he died in 1898, just as the sun was setting on the Victorians and their empire.

Though he was exceedingly gifted scholastically, young Carroll seemed to have been bored and unhappy with all of his accomplishments and positions in the Victorian milieu. He apparently was just strolling through life, until 1856, when a new Dean, Henry Liddell, arrived at Oxford University along with his wife and three young daughters, Lorina, Edith, and *Alice*.

Now, I don't know what *you* do for recreation, but this learned man of mathematics and deacon of the Church of England, married and with several children of his own, chose to spend a considerable amount of his time rowing these three preteen girls up a local river and back down again. During the ten-mile journey, Carroll made up clever stories with which to entertain his charges.

One of these tales was about a little girl named *Alice*, who was enchanted by a hurrying White Rabbit, and who fell down a rabbit hole while following him. It seemed to be a special favorite of the real little *Alice* Liddell riding in Carroll's boat. She even asked him to write the story down for her, which he did.

Alice's Adventures in Wonderland was published in 1865, and soon everyone in Victorian England, including Queen Victoria, was talking about it and its fantastic collection of characters and situations. In addition to Alice and the White Rabbit, there were the Caterpillar, the grinning Cheshire Cat ("We are all mad here"), the March Hare, The Mad Hatter, the Queen of Hearts ("Off with their heads"), the Mock Turtle, and the Gryphon.

This so-called children's book contained sophisticated double entendres, advanced mathematical concepts, references to sexual fantasies, derogatory statements about religious ceremonies, talk of drug use, and in my opinion thinly-veiled pedophilia.

In spite of these items, "Alice in Wonderland," as it came to be called, was a smash hit! It was a sensation in Victorian England from 1865 to the present day and in many foreign countries as well.

QUESTION: Into how many languages do you suppose this "children's book" has been translated?

ANSWER: Into 125 languages to date, and it has never been out of print! Try reading it once more, when the children are asleep.

Dr. Elizabeth Blackwell: "Excuse Me, Ma'am, Is the Doctor In?"

You'll be proud to know that On This Day, Elizabeth Blackwell became a medical doctor. What's so great about that, you ask? Well, it just so happens that Elizabeth Blackwell was the very *first* woman to receive a degree as a doctor of medicine from an American school. It happened On This Day, January 23, 1849. And thereby hangs a tale!

She was an immigrant, having been born in Bristol, England, part of a family of nine children. The Blackwells arrived in the United States in 1832, when Elizabeth was eleven years old.

The young girl seemed always to have been enamored by the practice of medicine. As she grew to maturity, she even "read medicine" by working at local hospitals and doctors' offices in Cincinnati, where she lived.

Elizabeth studied under the tutelage of her doctor-employers, voraciously reading every medical text she could lay her hands on. All agreed that she had the makings of a fine physician, except for one thing. She was a *woman* and no woman had ever been admitted to, much less graduated from, any American school of medicine.

But the determined Miss Blackwell would not be denied. She had already applied to a total of twenty-nine medical schools for admission. They all said, "No, we do not admit women." Finally, she fired off application number thirty to a tiny medical college in upstate New York.

The faculty and administration there were deeply perplexed about what to do with her application. They could not bring themselves to make a decision on the matter, so they decided to let the all-male student body decide.

Most of the boys thought it was some kind of a joke, and so they jovially voted "yes" on her admission to medical school. Joke or not, Elizabeth Blackwell was in.

She worked night and day to make the most of her hard-won opportunity. To everyone else's surprise, Elizabeth Blackwell graduated at the head of her class and immediately set off on an outstanding medical career.

She and her sister Emily, who had followed her into the medical profession, were the subjects of much ridicule in the United States. But when they returned to their native England, they were received as heroines. Elizabeth eventually founded the New York Infirmary for Women and Children and was primary in the formation of its Medical College for Women.

As time went on, Elizabeth Blackwell became a pioneer in preventative medicine and in the promotion of antisepsis and hygiene in the treatment of women. Her career marked an historic step forward in modern medicine and in women's liberation from the shackles of the past.

QUESTION: What was the name of that pioneering New York state school from which Elizabeth Blackwell got her medical degree?

ANSWER: It was then called Geneva Medical College, but is now a part of Hobart and William Smith Colleges in Geneva, New York, right on the shore of lovely Lake Geneva, one of the Finger Lakes.

FEBRUARY

Bare-Knuckle Boxing: Put Up Your Dukes and Fight Like a Man!

Good day, boxing fans! This is the anniversary of the last official bare-knuckle boxing contest in America.

ON THIS DAY, February 27, 1890, two relative unknowns, Danny Needham and Patsy Kerrigan, fought the final sanctioned bare-knuckle fight.

Boxing, of course, has been around for thousands of years. The earliest recognized fights of this type occurred in Greece in 688 BC, during the original Olympic games. In those days, the combatants were not only bare-knuckled but they were also completely bare all over! No ladies allowed.

The Olympians eventually used strips of soft ox-hide to protect their hands. Later the Romans, who were noted for their brutality, put iron and lead into the wrappings and sometimes even added the final sadistic touch with the addition of iron-studded gloves! So much for early civilization.

By the beginning of the 1700s, clandestine boxing contests began appearing in Great Britain featuring Irish vs. English pugilists. These were pretty barbarous affairs featuring bare-knuckled punching, wrestling, and kicking, topped off with no weight restrictions, no set number of rounds or length thereof . . . and no rest periods! The winner was the last man standing.

All of this "entertainment" for the English sporting classes came to an end about 1743, when rules governing most of the preceding practices were put into place in England. Prize fighting was of course still done in semi-secret locations. Sometimes there were not even any formal rings, just the patrons gathered round the fighters and "let 'em go at it!" Fights could end by a knockout, by capitulation, or by sudden police intervention!

Then the Marquis of Queensbury rules came to England in 1867; they were adopted in the United States by 1890. The new rules spelled the demise of bare-knuckle boxing since they required the use of padded boxing gloves; no wrestling, biting, or kicking; three-minute rounds, and a ten-second stand-up rule after a knockdown; and allowed only thirty seconds for the fighter's handler to bring him "up to scratch" to continue the fight.

John L. Sullivan was the last US bare-knuckle champion, but he was soon demolished by the boxing skills of "Gentleman Jim" Corbett. That was in 1892, when the first title fight under the new rules took over. But I digress.

Back to the last of the unknowns of the bare-knuckle era who fought that final match ON THIS DAY, February 27, 1890.

QUESTION: How many rounds did that Needham-Kerrigan fight go?

ANSWER: After *100* brutal rounds and *six and one-half* uninterrupted hours of brawling, the fight was declared a *draw*!

W. K. Kellogg: Now That's Downright Corny

It was ON THIS DAY, February 26, 1852, when John Kellogg was born. He was the older brother of W.K. Kellogg, whose name now adorns millions of Corn Flakes boxes.

John was a medical doctor and the somewhat eccentric head of his own sanitarium. Brother W.K. served him as a bookkeeper.

In most homes in post-Civil-War America, breakfast usually consisted of several fried eggs, large hunks of buttered bread, some kind of fried meat, fried mush, sometimes a large slice of pie, with several cups of black coffee to wash it down.

The Kellogg sanitarium had been set up to accommodate and educate people who wished to adopt a healthier lifestyle and a better diet. Together, the Kelloggs preached a regimen of exercise, fresh air, and the idea of a strict vegetarian diet inherited from their Seventh-Day Adventist parents.

"Doctor John," as he was known, also espoused other more astounding and some even revolting theories leading to his idea of perfect health. Among his better ideas were efforts to develop new "health foods" to replace those legendary heavy breakfasts.

In 1894, he and brother W.K., who despised each other, nonetheless jointly developed a method for successfully baking and then flaking a boiled and dried wheat and corn mixture. Dr. John was quite pleased with the invention, and apparently so were the patients in the sanitarium. They were gobbling up the new breakfast flakes. But brother W.K. insisted on further enhancing Dr. John's version of the new cereal. He wanted to sugar-coat the flakes! This was the end as far as Dr. John was concerned. He banished W.K. back to the books, and the sanitarium returned to the business at hand.

The story might have ended there, but it turned out that W.K. was of a more entrepreneurial bent and more interested in getting rich than his brother was. W.K. bought or stole (the stories vary) the idea and recipe for what was to become Kellogg's Corn Flakes; severed his connection with the sanitarium books; and the rest is history, more or less.

Except that W.K.'s action was followed by a lawsuit instituted by Dr. John with many nasty words passing back and forth. It soon came to a predictable end.

Dr. John went back to the sanitarium. W.K. emblazoned the family name and *his* initials on the cereal box, and made millions. The brothers never spoke to each other again!

QUESTION: In what Michigan city did all this turmoil occur?

ANSWER: Battle Creek, Michigan, was and is the place, home today of both Kellogg and Post cereals. And it all began with the birth of John Kellogg on February 26, 1852.

Rotary International Breezes Past 100

Happy birthday to you. Happy birthday to you. Happy birthday, dear Rotary, happy birthday to you.

America's first service club was born ON THIS DAY, February 23, 1905. It was a cold and blustery evening in Chicago. A raw wind was blowing off Lake Michigan. Paul P. Harris, a corporate lawyer for nine years in the Windy City, turned up his coat collar as he walked down Dearborn Street toward history. Paul was lonely, feeling overwhelmed by the isolation of the big city, and he clearly saw the wisdom of the idea of helping others. He and three other noncompetitive businessmen met that night in Room 711 of the Unity Building. They were Harris, a lawyer; Schiele, a coal dealer; Loehr, a mining engineer; and Shorey, a merchant tailor. Not much connection among their businesses, but the idea was that men in business could be personal friends and help each other in matters of commerce.

One of the four, who loved music, jumped up on a chair (I am not making this up) and enthusiastically suggested that they sing! Instead of falling on the floor laughing, they all burst forth in song, as do many Rotary clubs to this day. Finally, it dawned upon the assembled four that perhaps they should meet on a regular basis . . . and thus was born the world's first Rotary club.

It must have been one of those "Hey, let's form a club" inspirational outbursts that was later immortalized in the Andy Hardy movies, but form a club they did, naming it Rotary because their original plan was to meet "in rotation" at the various places of business of the members.

I'm sure that no Rotarian ON THIS DAY in 1905 ever dreamed that the idea set in motion on that windy February night in Chicago would someday be accepted by men and women around the world. But it has been. Five years after Rotary's founding, there were sixteen Rotary clubs and 1,500 Rotarians! That same year, Rotary went international with a club in Winnipeg, Canada.

On its 100th birthday, Rotary International boasted a presence in 160 countries with 1,219,532 members who belong to 31,936 clubs, including four in Franklin County, Pennsylvania (Chambersburg, Waynesboro, Greencastle, and Mercersburg).

But numbers do not tell the entire story. Rotary has become a force for peace through its Rotary International Foundation, which sponsors worldwide high school student exchanges; vocational, undergraduate, and graduate scholarships; and international vocational exchange programs for teams of established young professional men and women. It also sponsors a worldwide polio-eradication program and a vast health, hunger, and humanity effort to alleviate many of the scourges of mankind. Thus, Rotary works to make life better for all our fellow men and women.

QUESTION: What do you suppose was the very first humanitarian project carried out by the world's first Rotary club?

ANSWER: They built a public restroom for the hard-pressed citizens of Chicago!

The Impeachment of President Johnson

This is a truly historic day. ON THIS DAY February 24, 1868, something happened to the head of the US government that had never happened before and wouldn't happen again for 131 more years! The first post-Civil-War president of the United States was served with articles of impeachment. Please note that "served" means he was charged with high crimes and misdemeanors, but not as yet tried and convicted or exonerated by the court.

I am sure that by this time you know that I'm referring to President Andrew Johnson (and to President Bill Clinton 131 years later). Vice President Johnson had suddenly and without preparation been thrust into the presidency by the bullet that took the life of our sixteenth president, Abraham Lincoln. Johnson was actually a Southern Democrat, running with Republican Abraham Lincoln as part of a National Union Party designed to end the Civil War (and to get elected).

Johnson had done it all; he had been a town councilman, mayor, and member of both houses of the Tennessee legislature. Then he went on to Washington as a member of the US House of Representatives . . . governor of Tennessee . . . US senator . . . military governor of Tennessee (having been appointed by Lincoln early in the war) . . . then vice-president of the United States (for six weeks), and finally, president. Not bad for a man with no formal schooling who could not read or write until he was an adult! However, his troubles did not really begin until he became president.

He, like Lincoln, favored treating the defeated Southern states with compassion. The Congress, dominated by "radical" Republicans, wanted to punish the Confederacy. For three long years during his presidential term, the executive and legislative branches fought to carry out their opposed

Reconstruction ideas and to establish supremacy over the other. The House and the Senate passed laws; President Johnson vetoed them. And then often the Congress would vote to make them law, overriding his veto.

One of the biggest political thorns in Johnson's side was Lincoln's "left over" Secretary of War, Edwin M. Stanton. The president tried to fire Stanton; Congress passed a special "Tenure of Office Act" designed to prevent Stanton's dismissal by the president. Johnson fired him anyway and thereby triggered the impeachment process.

The trial was held in the well of the Senate chamber, with Supreme Court Chief Justice Salmon P. Chase presiding. (You know him; he's the one whose picture is on the $10,000 bill.) It dragged on until May 16, 1868, when a vote for the acquittal of President Johnson was brought in.

QUESTION: Do you know by how many votes was he finally acquitted?

ANSWER: You are right! One vote was the margin of victory for Andrew Johnson . . . thirty-five guilty . . . nineteen for acquittal! Remember that the next time you enter a voting booth or are asked for your opinion on an important matter.

The Senate becomes a court of
impeachment for President Johnson.

Samuel Colt: Colt, Colt, Colt. (Yes, it was a Colt repeater)

The funeral was spectacular! The deceased was only forty-seven years of age, but he had raced through a tumultuous life and was consequentially well-known.

And he was rich, always a big attention-getter.

The pomp and circumstance of the funeral was almost like the last act of some grand opera. The dear departed, who was a spectacularly successful manufacturer, was preceded to his private resting place by his personal German-style band, composed of his own German-immigrant factory craftsmen.

Fifteen-hundred other bereaved, crepe-draped workmen were followed by most of the inhabitants of Hartford, Connecticut, all on their way to the deceased's ducal mansion called Armsmear, which overlooked the Connecticut River.

Then followed his personal military guard company, Company A of the 17th Regiment, Connecticut Volunteers, topped off by the smart-looking Putnam Phalanx in their brilliant blue Continental uniforms.

After a simple Episcopal service, the workers formed two lines. The Putnam Phalanx stepped off with drums muffled, colors draped, and arms reversed, to deposit the body in the grave near his private lake. Volley after volley of shots rang out from repeating rifles in salute to the great man. The date was January 14, 1862.

QUESTION: Who was this fabulous person? P.T. Barnum? No. Mark Twain? No. Some former US president? No. A fallen hero of the Mexican or early Civil War? No. Maybe an inventive genius who had discovered the fountain of youth? Well, no, not quite. If you don't already know his famous name, reread this page. There are a few clues to his identity.

ANSWER: He was "Colonel" Samuel Colt, America's first hugely successful munitions maker, inventor of the Colt five—and six-shot revolvers and father of the Colt Peacemaker, called "the gun that won the West." Some even say his repeating firearms won the Civil War for the Union forces.

Colt left behind a thirty-six-year-old widow, two sons (one legitimate, one otherwise) and fifteen million dollars to keep them in the style to which he had accustomed them.

It was ON THIS DAY, February 25, 1836, that young Sam Colt received patents from Great Britain, France, and the United States on his six-shot pistol. The road to success was now open, and he seldom looked back or reflected on the moral implications of dealing in weapons of death and destruction.

MARCH

The USS *Constitution*, "Old Ironsides,"
is the Navy's oldest commissioned warship.
Credit: U.S. Navy photo by Journalist Seaman Joe Burgess

The US Navy is Born:
Anchors Aweigh, A Way Back

Well, let's see. The actual date we are remembering is March 27, 1794, the day on which the US Navy was born—or, more accurately, the date on which it was re-born.

During the American Revolution as many as fifty war ships, known as the Continental Navy, had sailed under the colors of the new nation. But the battered Continental Navy had ceased operations at the close of the Revolutionary War and the remaining vessels were put, by Congressional order, into the care of one Robert Morris, a prominent banker.

Now what do you suppose he did with them? Well, the war was over, so he did what any banker would do: he sold them to the highest bidder! The Navy was essentially out of business by 1785.

But peace without strength does not usually last very long. In October 1793 trouble came from an unexpected quarter—the Barbary Coast of Africa. Algerian pirates had seized three American merchant ships and enslaved their crews! More trouble was yet to come.

Moving with unaccustomed speed, the US Congress approved The Naval Act of 1794 on March 27 of that year, authorizing the construction of six naval frigates, but with a clause that suspended the new naval construction in case the United States had signed a satisfactory peace treaty with Algiers before they were built.

Action and reaction were not long in coming. On September 5, 1795, a treaty of peace was signed with Algeria, releasing sixty-five American sailors from slavery. So the naval construction was stopped.

However, there was continuing trouble with Barbary pirates, those based in Tripoli. So Congress passed the Naval Act of 1796, which authorized the completion of the three frigates, which had first been authorized in 1794. Get it?

Later that same year, we scared (and bribed) the pasha of Tripoli into concluding a peace treaty with the United States. Congress breathed a sigh of relief, for now those ships would apparently not be needed. Stop the shipbuilding!

However, all was not yet "wine and roses." Now that the French Revolution had ended, our erstwhile friends in Paris became our enemies, and in 1797 began searching and seizing American merchant ships on the high seas. So the continuing need for naval protection finally convinced the Congress that a strong navy was a desirable thing for a nation to possess.

Construction of the ships authorized in 1794 continued apace, with both USS *Constitution* and USS *Constellation* actually being launched in 1797, followed by a long line of illustrious war ships and naval heroes.

And that is how March 27, 1794, came to be known as the date the US Navy began. Happy birthday to all of you "gobs" (and "gobettes") out there.

QUESTION: Which US president authorized the building of those first six ships under the Naval Act of 1794?

ANSWER: Why, George Washington, of course. The same one who had previously warned us to avoid "foreign entanglements."

Henry VIII: What a Way to Run a Church!

Aah, what a small world it was ON THIS DAY. How different it would have been if only England's King Henry VIII's first wife, Catherine of Aragon, had produced a castle full of sturdy sons instead of one daughter who was later to be crowned (briefly) as Mary I of England.

But Henry wanted a son . . . a son . . . a *son* . . . to inherit the English throne. And Henry was willing to go to any lengths to get one.

First, he tried to have his marriage to Catherine of Aragon annulled.

Heck, she had been "left to him" as his brother Henry VII's widow—she came right along with the kingdom and the crown. But after years of no sons who lived, Henry wanted a new wife.

Thomas Cardinal Wolsey, Henry's ambitious chief minister, took the royal problem directly to Pope Clement VII, asking him to annul the king's marriage.

"Absolutely not," said the pope. And that is when the stuff hit the fan.

Henry dismissed Wolsey, shoved wife Catherine aside, and bade Parliament declare that the Roman Catholic Church and the pope no longer had any authority in England. Having gone this far, Henry appointed himself as head of the Church of England, made Thomas Cranmer archbishop of Canterbury, and then summarily ordered the new archbishop to declare Henry's marriage to Catherine to be null and void (which Cranmer did). Wow!

Henry was now free to marry Catherine's maid-in-waiting, Anne Boleyn, who was already "in waiting" with a hoped-for male heir fathered by Henry.

Alas, the "male heir" turned out to be a female named Elizabeth, much to Henry's dissatisfaction. The marriage itself lasted only three years, until Henry had Anne beheaded!

She was followed to the altar and to the throne by Jane Seymour . . . Anne of Cleves . . . Catherine Howard . . . and finally Catherine Parr, the only wife to outlive Henry VIII, and she did that by only one year.

All this happened back in the early to mid sixteenth century in England.

QUESTION: What happened ON THIS DAY in 1966 to make it religiously noteworthy?

ANSWER: Well, it took a long time to arrange it, but on March 23, 1966, the Roman Catholic pope and the Church of England's archbishop of Canterbury actually met face to face for the first time in 400 years, to discuss the separation of the two churches. Nothing much came of the meeting, but hey, it's a start!

The First Women's Basketball Game: The Net Result, Women in on the Ground Floor

On This Day, March 22, 1893, a remarkable thing happened. Girls—young women really—hit the gym floor at Smith College in Northampton, Massachusetts, and began to play an organized basketball game for the first time. Now you may not think this to be remarkable, considering that basketball (for boys, naturally) had been invented shortly before in nearby Springfield, Massachusetts.

But the rules for girls were, however, somewhat different from those observed by the boys. A Smith College phys. ed. teacher, Senda Berenson, made up the rules of girls' basketball to suit her own purposes. Her aim was to push teamwork and cooperation among all the players, even with those on the opposing team! Imagine that. No stars on her teams.

Oh yes, there were nine players on each girls' team and the basketball court was divided into three zones, with three players assigned to each zone. This was important, for Coach Berenson's rules explicitly stated that no girl could leave her zone! She could only hold the ball for three seconds, and was allowed to dribble the ball just three times before passing it. And there was to be no grabbing of the ball from another player.

Doesn't this sound exciting? Well, you don't know the half of it. To wit: they used an old, beat-up soccer ball in the game, a real peach basket (with bottom intact), and boys and men were *strictly* forbidden from being in the gym while the game and the girls were in motion.

Sound strange? Not really, for this was 1893 and (1) the college wouldn't spend the extra money needed for a real basketball for the women; (2) ditto for a hoop and net to be used as a goal. It was even necessary, after each score, for someone to climb a stepladder and retrieve the ball, until they finally got smart and kicked the bottom out of the peach basket. This, by the way, is reputed to be the origin of the name of the game of basketball. And (3) no self-respecting young lady of the late 1890s would have appeared in public before any male while "provocatively" attired in billowing bloomers and long-sleeved woolen blouses. They even went so far as to cover and seal the windows and lock the doors when the game was in progress!

It was kind of a makeshift first game, but the awakening desires of women for equality would not be denied. Thus ON THIS DAY, March 22, 1893, the first collegiate basketball game was played at Smith College.

QUESTION: Who were the two teams, and who won?

ANSWER: It was a strictly intramural game—freshmen versus sophomores. The frosh won 5-4 in a spirited contest enjoyed by all . . . women!

Senda Berenson made sure women,
too, could aim for "nothing but net."

The Spanish Civil War: Some Folks Just Can't Wait for the Main Event

ON THIS DAY, March 28, 1939, most of Europe was still at peace.

Though just five months away from the beginning of World War II, a bloody civil war was just ending in a devastated Spain. As it turned out, the Spanish Civil War was something of a rehearsal for World War II. The Communists aided the losing Loyalist Republican cause and the Nazi German and Fascist Italian governments backed Generalissimo Francisco Franco and his victorious Nationalist Rebel forces.

It's hard to believe that the once mighty Spanish Empire—the nation that had sent Christopher Columbus to search for the Indies; the country that had conquered and explored all of South and Central America, Mexico, Florida, and most of the southwestern United States; the nation that had launched the mighty Spanish Armada against England; the country that had enjoyed the benefits of billions in gold and slaves from their conquered territories—was now torn apart and nearly destroyed by a home-grown war.

The decline of modern Spain really began with their final colonial defeats by the United States in Cuba, the Philippines, Guam, and Puerto Rico at the end of the nineteenth century. From then on, political life in Spain was like a roller coaster. The Liberals—along with the trade unions and the regions demanding complete independence—vied with the Conservatives, the monarchy, the Army, and the Roman Catholic Church for control of the country.

Finally, a military coup seized power in 1923 and held it until 1930, when Republican election victories overthrew the military government and forced the king to leave the country, though not to abdicate. The Republicans then ruled Spain for five years, dealing with widespread poverty and great unrest among the Spanish citizenry. Internal political divisions were ever widening. The army, the monarchists, and Roman Catholic groups made up the Right. The Communists, Socialists, trade unions, Anarchists, and assorted other Liberal groups inhabited the Left and Center-Left of the political spectrum.

Thus the stage was set for civil war in Spain. It began in July 1936, when the army revolted against the elected, but largely ineffective, Republican government. Things quickly got out of hand, and soon a full-scale war erupted, with General Francisco Franco acting as the Nationalist army's chief of staff.

Nazi Germany and Fascist Italy weighed in on the side of the Nationalists, taking the opportunity to preview some of their newest military hardware. Communist Russia, along with Leftist volunteers from many European and American communities, supported the Loyalists.

The war lasted nearly three years. Up to one million lost their lives. Most Spanish cities were severely damaged. Franco became dictator for life. The Roman Catholic Church remained in control of people's spiritual lives. And eventually a figurehead monarch returned to the Spanish throne in 1975 after the death of Franco.

QUESTION: Would you happen to know the king's name?

ANSWER: He is named Juan Carlos I and he is still on the Spanish throne! The Spanish Civil War ended ON THIS DAY, March 28, 1939.

APRIL

In God We Trust

No, this is not just another Civil War story, but isn't it strange how war brings out both the best and the worst in people and nations?

ON THIS DAY, April 22, 1864, the United States was locked in a bitter civil war. Ulysses S. Grant had been named general-in-chief of the Northern armies. Gettysburg was almost a year in the past. The war seemed to be at a stalemate. Thousands of Confederate and Union soldiers lay lifeless on battlefields across the nation. Both belligerents were eager for a resolution of the conflict. It was at this opportune time that the US Congress thought it would be a good idea to state the nation's reliance on divine help and guidance. So the lawmakers quickly authorized the minting of a coin with the phrase "In God We Trust" engraved upon it.

The production of the new coin was authorized ON THIS DAY, April 22, 1864, by Congress to alleviate the serious coin shortages caused by the war, as well as to seek any available divine intervention in deciding the conflict. James Barton Longacre, the chief engraver of the US Mint, was called upon to do the design. He had also engraved the very popular Indian-head cent and the shield nickel. As a matter of fact, Longacre seemed to have been so rushed with the production of the new coin that he simply redid his shield nickel design for the new copper piece. The obverse (front) of the coin bears the date, a shield with a ribbon over it bearing the new motto "In God We Trust," plus various arrows and leafy branches (olive branches?) surrounding it.

QUESTION: What was the denomination of this new Civil-War-era coin?

ANSWER: It was a two-cent piece! What, you didn't know that we ever had a two-cent coin? Well, it was only issued for nine years, but that catchy phrase "In God We Trust" took on a life of its own, continuing to this day. Check out news of the half-dime and the three-cent piece also in circulation at that time.

Social Security Begins

Ah! What a glorious spring day. On This Day in 1937, the weather was good, but the financial situation in the United States was not. Many persons were still out of work, and some of those with jobs were characterized as "the working poor."

In those days, having a job was often close to being a matter of life or death. Families were large, and people were frequently hungry. People who were sick sometimes got free medical care from compassionate doctors, but more often they resorted to home remedies . . . or they just died!

There was no expectation of retirement among the general population, and hardly a retirement or nursing home was available. When Mom and Pop got too physically old to work or to care for themselves any longer, they had to move in with the kids, if they were able to take them in. Absent the possibility of family care, many lived on the street, begging for sustenance!

As you can see, 1937 was not one of the great years in American history. We were ever so slowly emerging from the Great Depression. Franklin Delano Roosevelt, who was then in the middle of his second term as president, was doing everything that Congress would allow to get a law providing comprehensive care for the elderly, handicapped, and unemployed.

After fourteen contentious months, Congress finally passed the Social Security Act over conservative cries of "It will ruin our institutions!" The date was August 14, 1935.

On This Day, April 27, 1937, the nation's very first Social Security check was mailed out. I don't know to whom it was sent, or for what amount, but I'm sure that the recipient must have thought it contained "Pennies from Heaven."

It was a ray of hope, a helping hand extended by a caring government. No wonder FDR was four times elected president of the United States.

It wasn't included in the original Social Security Act of 1935, but thirty years later, Congress added a system for those over age sixty-five to receive hospital and related health-insurance benefits under the Social Security program.

QUESTION: What was this new benefit called?

ANSWER: Medicare, which is not to be confused with the state-run Medicaid program for the poor.

Guglielmo Marconi's Inventions

I always had trouble with his name until I tied it in with "Tickle Me Elmo" and then I could zip it right off as "Googlie-elmo" Marconi. Anyway, he was born On This Day in 1874 and he filled a very important niche in all of our lives.

Guglielmo Marconi was the second son of a wealthy Italian nobleman. He had a brilliant mind and a passion for investigating the secrets of physical and electrical science. And he did it all without ever attending a public school! He was privately educated, of course, and by age twenty-one was actively pursuing his interest in electric telegraphy entirely on his own, using his father's estate, a private yacht, and a rented ocean liner as his bases of operations.

Like most inventors of every age, he had a restless mind that seized upon the experiments and successes of others as the basis for the further improvements of his work.

When I mentioned electric telegraphy, most readers probably thought of "dot-dash" and the miles of wire strung across the countryside by its inventor, Samuel F.B. Morse, and his successors during the mid-1800s. By the time that Marconi was born in 1874, the world was already demanding something better.

And boy, did he give it to them!

Marconi had the idea that it ought to be possible to send signals and even voices through the air without any connecting wires. And this is just what he produced! In 1895 he sent wireless signals over a distance of one and a half miles. By 1899 wireless signals were winging their way across the English Channel. And on an historic December day in 1901, Marconi transmitted the first wireless signals between England and St. John's, Newfoundland, a distance of 2,100 nautical miles.

Soon Marconi wireless devices became standard issue on transatlantic ships, and were credited several times with saving lives in emergency situations.

Even the ill-fated *Titanic* sent out Marconi wireless signals in a fruitless call for help before sinking in 1912.

Honors and awards poured in on the Italian inventor. He was honored with the Nobel Prize in physics in 1909, and there was yet much more to come!

QUESTION: Do you know what additional great inventions flowed out of these early successes by Marconi?

ANSWER: radio, both AM and FM; television; and radar! Other brilliant men share the credit for these later successes, but Guglielmo Marconi was the catalyst for their achievements. And he was born ON THIS DAY, April 25, 1874.

A replica of the *Bounty*

Mutiny on the *Bounty*

On This Day, April 28, 1789, an unthinkable event occurred. There was an insurrection, a mutiny if you will, on His Majesty's Ship *Bounty*. The British ship and its crew were in the South Seas to pick up a load of breadfruit trees from Tahiti. The admiralty back in London thought the trees might be replanted in the British islands of the Caribbean to inexpensively feed British slaves there.

It turned out that when the *Bounty* weighed anchor in Tahiti, the breadfruit trees were five months from being ripe enough for shipment. So the merry seamen of the *Bounty* swam ashore, claimed native "wives," and proclaimed themselves to be ready for an idyllic life in the sunny South Seas. It was fun while it lasted, but on April 4, 1789, the trees were ready, but the sailors were not. After rounding up the crew at gunpoint, Captain Bligh and the HMS *Bounty* set sail for the Caribbean.

For a long time I thought that the exciting 1935 movie *Mutiny on the Bounty* was just historical fiction. I still don't know what the real Captain William Bligh looked like, but in my mind's eye he'll always have Charles Laughton's sneering countenance.

Well, to get on with the story, On This Day, the mutineers, led by Clark Gable (well, really by Fletcher Christian) took over HMS *Bounty* from the allegedly tyrannical rule of Captain Bligh, setting him and eighteen of his loyal seamen adrift in a rowboat containing a sextant, a few days worth of food and water, and four cutlasses!

Now bear in mind that mutiny on the high seas was a capital crime, punishable by hanging from the nearest yardarm. No wonder then that the nine mutineers sailed toward an uninhabited dot of land in the ocean some 5,000 miles east of Australia known as Pitcairn Island, tossed the breadfruit overboard, scuttled the ship to avoid detection by vengeful British authorities, and settled in to enjoy life in the South Seas.

However, it didn't turn out that way. On their way to Pitcairn Island, the *Bounty* again stopped at Tahiti, picking up six additional men and twelve women. Let's see: fifteen total men and twelve women—ah, yes, that must have been the root of the tragedy. After a few years only one man had survived, and he was happily ruling over a peaceful and contented colony of twelve women! I don't know what happened to the other men, but I can guess.

QUESTION: What happened to Captain Bligh and the eighteen seamen who were adrift in a rowboat in the South Pacific?

ANSWER: Incredibly, Bligh and company, after suffering forty-seven days of extreme hardship and sailing over 3,600 miles, landed safely in Australia! And, in true storybook fashion, Captain Bligh was appointed governor of New South Wales, Australia, and later was promoted to the rank of vice-admiral in the Royal Navy. The seventeen surviving seamen became colonists Down Under and almost everyone lived happily ever after.

And to think it all began ON THIS DAY, April 28, 1789.

MAY

The north face of world's highest mountain, Everest
Credit: Adeh DeSandies

Mount Everest: You're the Top

It was ON THIS DAY, May 29, 1953, that the unlikely pairing of a New Zealand beekeeper and a Sherpa Mt. Everest guide combined to do what no man had done before.

On that day both Edmund Hillary and Tenzing Norgay were full-fledged climbing members of a British expedition that was under considerable political pressure to become the first to climb Mt. Everest. Thirty-four-year-old Hillary was not the leader, just one of the climbers. As a matter of fact, the longtime head of the British expedition had just been sacked in favor of a military man with a great deal of organizational experience.

There was so much pressure because favorable climbing weather was fast slipping away. Great Britain was about to crown a new monarch, and the powers that be wanted a British victory on Mt. Everest to coincide with coronation day for Elizabeth II. Someone said, "Make it so, Number One," and the race was on.

The British team included all of the experienced mountaineers who could be found in that part of Asia. Edmund Hillary had been climbing ever since WWII had ended and, as a matter of fact, he had "warmed up" by twice climbing part way up the forbidding ice cliffs of Everest earlier that year. He was determined to make it to the top in '53.

Thirty-nine-year-old Tenzing Norgay, an experienced mountaineer, had spent much of his year herding sheep and goats in the higher reaches of the Himalayas. Actually, he would hire out to any expedition willing to pay him for professional guide services.

The expedition made it to the eighth camp at 28,000 feet. At this point the assault teams consisted of only two men each, and Hillary and Norgay were third and fourth in line. The first two men were off for the top, getting within 300 feet of the summit when their specially designed oxygen equipment failed. They very reluctantly returned to base camp, and our two heroes were given the nod.

Hillary and Norgay cautiously climbed to 28,750 feet and camped for the night. At six the next morning, they thawed their boots with a small gas stove and at 6:30 started for the top. It took them five hours to go the last 250 feet! Finally, at 11:30 a.m., they made it, celebrating by hugging and shaking hands, taking pictures, planting flags in the snow, and picking up souvenir stones at the summit. They were the first to stand five and a half miles above sea level, at the top of the world!

QUESTION: What did they do with all of the fame and money that their achievement bestowed upon them?

ANSWER: Tenzing Norgay (who died in 1986) set up a professional mountaineering federation school in India to help those who wished to continue challenging the mountain. He was awarded the George Medal from Great Britain.

Edmund Hillary (who died in 2008) was knighted by a delighted young queen. He used his money and influence to set up a grammar school in India to educate Sherpa children.

Bonnie and Clyde: Stop, in the Name of the Law

May 23, 1934. It was the depth of the Great Depression, when the song "Brother, Can You Spare a Dime?" was a cry for help. The American people were disillusioned, discouraged, and desperate. Some searched for their next meal, some for the mortgage payment, some for a bit of the self-respect that had blown away with the great dust storm . . . the stock market crash of '29 . . . the loss of their job . . . and the demeaning necessity of standing in a bread line.

America was looking for heroes, bigger-than-life heroes who would stand up to the law and give their admirers some second-hand thrills. Anything to take their minds off the terrible Depression and the mundane, boring lives it had sentenced them to.

Bonnie and Clyde filled the bill to a "T." They were glamorous, exciting, young people—the new Robin Hoods of the Old West. For nearly two years, they had terrorized banks and stores by robbing, plundering, and murdering their way to this climactic day in 1934.

The final act of the tragedy took place on a rural road in the bayou country of Louisiana. Bonnie and Clyde were racing along a dusty byway, driving a stolen nearly new Ford Deluxe sedan (always their getaway car of choice), when everything came to a calamitous finish. In an instant, the sporty Ford was converted into a death car with dozens of holes from 45s, 38s, and high-powered shotguns decorating the scene.

Bonnie and Clyde had driven into a police ambush, and they richly deserved their fate. But down-and-out America grieved mightily for them. They were national folk heroes. The two who took on the establishment and won—for a while, anyway.

We've been calling them Bonnie and Clyde as if they were one, and indeed they appeared to have been deeply in love. But they were, of course, two individuals, each with a different last name.

QUESTION: Do you know those names?

ANSWER: They were Bonnie *Parker* and Clyde *Barrow*—born into poverty, living lives of desperation, dying at the hands of the law. It seems that their motto paralleled a popular expression of the day, "Live fast, die young, and leave a good-looking corpse." But I'm very sure that they wouldn't have traded those wild two years for anything else in the world. For they were "Bonnie and Clyde" and they died ON THIS DAY, May 23, 1934.

Legendary outlaws Bonnie Parker and Clyde Barrow
Credit: Photo by one of the Barrow gang

P.G.T. Beauregard: the Man Who Started the Civil War

P.G.T. Beauregard was born ON THIS DAY, May 28, 1818, on a large plantation just outside New Orleans.

Who, you may ask, was this Southerner with the yard-long name that takes five minutes to say Southern style?

Well, I'll tell you. P.G.T. Beauregard, in his prime, was many things, most notably a skilled general in the employ of the Confederate States of America. And yet most of us have never heard of him!

Look up his picture and you will immediately see visions of the Old South: swirling cotillion dances, huge plantation houses, men taking their cigars and bourbon on the veranda, remembering heroic stands on far-flung Civil War battlefields. That vision would be right on for P.G.T. Beauregard, for he seemed to be the very model of a Confederate general.

Graduated in 1838 from West Point, standing second in his class, Beauregard went into the Regular Army and within ten years had become one of the real heroes of the US-Mexican War. He even served as superintendent of the US Military Academy at West Point for five days in early 1861 just before the outbreak of the Civil War.

But for P.G.T. Beauregard, the big news was yet to come. You may be interested to know that he was the man who began the Civil War . . . literally!

Brigadier General Beauregard, CSA, was in command of the Charleston Home Guards on April 12, 1861, leading a pack of spoiling-for-war Southerners who were facing the meager Union forces hunkered down in Charleston Harbor's Fort Sumter.

General Beauregard was the one who calmly said, "Gentlemen, you may fire when ready," backed up by the cheers and huzzahs of the watching Charleston citizenry. And the rest, as they say, is history.

But wait, there is more, *much* more!

Within three months of the surrender of Fort Sumter, Beauregard had been promoted to full general in the Confederate Army! He seemed to have had it all: the military education, the experience, the bravery, and the panache of a historic military figure. So what happened?

Well, to put it bluntly, he was a victim of Southern discrimination. A French Creole from Louisiana, he was a different sort of Southern gentleman—not quite like the English-bred Confederate President Jefferson Davis or General Robert E. Lee or most of the rest of the Confederate officer corps. In addition, P.G.T. Beauregard was vain, arrogant, and uncompromising. Sparks flew from the very beginning.

But he surely acquitted himself admirably during the war, most notably seizing Southern victory from defeat at First Bull Run, fighting bravely at Shiloh and in the defense of Corinth, Mississippi, and at Drewry's Bluff. He repeatedly defended Charleston from Union attacks and was instrumental in the defense of Richmond and Petersburg. But the top brass just didn't like him!

General Beauregard survived the Civil War, returning to his native Louisiana, serving as president of several railroads, entering politics as a Democrat, producing military writings, and even heading up the Louisiana Lottery!

P.G.T. Beauregard died in 1873, at nearly seventy-five years of age.

QUESTION: What do you suppose those famous initials P.G.T. stood for?

ANSWER: Pierre Gustave Toutant, of course. No wonder he used the initials—he was surely one of the "old school" of Southern Creole gentlemen.

We salute you, General P.G.T. Beauregard!

Who Owns Hong Kong?

Ah yes, lovely Hong Kong, whose name in Cantonese means "fragrant harbor." Crowded Hong Kong, with more than seven million mostly Chinese people living within its 428 square miles of land. Uncertain Hong Kong, which currently both is *and* isn't part of the Communist People's Republic of China. Rich Hong Kong, with a US $300 billion gross national product, some $42,000 (US dollars) per person living there!

Modern Hong Kong came into being because of opium. As a matter of fact, two wars were fought between the Chinese empire and Great Britain over the proposed sale and distribution in China of the powerful narcotic. Surprisingly enough, in this case the British were the bad guys. The knowing Chinese authorities of the Qing Dynasty had refused to allow importation of opium into China but the Brits, driven by a powerful profit motive, went to war in 1839 to force the drug upon the Chinese people! China lost that First Opium War and had to cede the island of Hong Kong to the "white devils."

After the Second Opium War in 1860, Great Britain obtained the adjoining Kowloon Peninsula from China and in 1898 sealed the deal for still more land (with a ninety-nine-year lease), thus adding the part of China known as the New Territories to the British Crown Colony of Hong Kong. Now Britain was ready for business. And business was good . . . all the way up to Christmas Day 1941, when victorious Japanese occupation troops made their triumphal march down Queen's Road in Hong Kong following the surrender of the British and Australian defenders.

Returned to Great Britain following World War II, Hong Kong almost immediately prospered as a safe haven for people and property fleeing the Communist revolution then raging in mainland China. Next, the restored British Crown Colony became nearly the only point of contact for trade with the emerging Communist People's Republic of China. The island bastion became a beehive of service-based, financial, banking, and diplomatic activities for most of Southeast Asia.

But, as usual, change was not long in coming to this volatile area. Great Britain's ninety-nine-year lease was set to run out in 1997, and by the 1980s this fact loomed ever larger over Hong Kong business and the touchy political relations between East and West. However, after extensive bargaining with the mainland Chinese, On This Day, May 27, 1985, the British government reaffirmed the 1898 lease agreement and promised to give Hong Kong back to China in 1997!

QUESTION: What do you suppose were the final terms extracted by the Brits as the price of turning Hong Kong back to the Chinese?

ANSWER: For the next fifty years (or so), Hong Kong is to be a "special administrative unit" within China, retaining its own currency, legal, and political systems but all under the "protection" of Chinese foreign affairs and defense systems. Ain't diplomacy grand?

The Great Auto Race

George Schuster was somewhere between St. Petersburg, Russia, and Berlin, Germany, ON THIS DAY, May 26, 1908. He was desperately driving a battered, mud-splattered 1907 Thomas Flyer automobile and pushing hard to be the winner of the $1,000 cash prize in the "Greatest Auto Race," invented and sponsored by the *New York Times* and Paris' *Le Matin* newspapers.

George had begun the year as a mechanic and jack of all trades working for the E.R. Thomas Motor Company of Buffalo, New York. On February 11, he got a phone call from the boss to be in New York City bright and early the next morning prepared to ride along on a little auto trip. "Pack light, you won't be gone too long," said Thomas, inventor of the Flyer.

On the morning of February 12, 1908, George Schuster was astounded to see 250,000 people wildly cheering the six spiffy-looking motorcars lined up on Broadway. "What's going on here?" he asked Thomas. The boss replied, "Why, this is the start of the great New York to Paris auto race, and you could win the $1,000 first prize."

The astonished Schuster climbed aboard, joining the driver, a dashing sportsman named Montague Roberts, and, of course a newsman from the *New York Times*. The six starting autos zoomed up Broadway at speeds exceeding thirty MPH! The Thomas Flyer, boasting the power of a four-cylinder, sixty-horsepower engine, thundered into the lead. Behind it came a Zust from Italy, a Protos from Germany, and three assorted cars from France.

They had originally hoped to see the West Coast in twenty-two days. As it turned out, it took forty-one days to reach San Francisco while driving through hub-cap-deep mud, extraordinary drifts of snow, and on nearly nonexistent US highways. However the Thomas Flyer found that it led the pack by eight days at that point.

Along the way to the West, the original driver of the Thomas car begged off in Cheyenne, Wyoming, citing a prior commitment. The *Times* reporter left in Chicago, calling the event "insanity." Various replacements came on board, but by the time they reached the West Coast, there was only George Schuster, another mechanic, plus a new reporter who came along for the ride.

They soon found that they had just completed the "easy" part of the trip. They were supposed to take a boat to Alaska, then drive over frozen rivers and dogsled trails to the Bering Strait and thence across Siberia to Paris! They tried it, but had to give up early on, finally rerouting the boat to Japan and then to Vladivostok, Russia. Schuster had now taken over as driver. He was also the chief mechanic, retuning the Flyer after each day's strenuous drive through snowstorms, sand storms, floods, and sub-zero temperatures—all without a windshield or a top on the car!

As it turned out, Schuster and the Thomas Flyer arrived in Paris on July 30, 1908, only to find to their dismay that the German Protos was already there, having arrived four days earlier. But our heroes were declared the winners nonetheless, the German team being penalized for various short cuts, such as shipping the Protos part way by rail, not going to Alaska, and somehow failing to drive some 3,246 miles of the journey.

It took them a few weeks to get it all sorted out, but the Thomas Flyer was finally declared the winner.

QUESTION: How many days do you suppose it took them to complete the New York to Paris trip?

ANSWER: It took "only" 169 days to travel about 22,000 miles from New York to Paris, the hard way. The German Protos was declared second, losing by twenty-six days. The Italians arrived at the finish line in September 1908. The French machines never made it home.

For some reason, Schuster did not collect his $1,000 prize until he was awarded it at a special Motor Club ceremony when he was ninety-five years old, just four years before his death. George Schuster did get the promise of a "lifetime" job with the Thomas Motor Company, but it went bankrupt just four years later.

JUNE

William Penn

ON THIS DAY, June 23, 1683, one William Penn signed a treaty of friendship and made an exchange of gifts with the Lenni-Lenape (or Delaware) Indians, who thought *they* owned what came to be known as the Province of Pennsylvania.

Today's Pennsylvanians live on some of those Indian lands, and yet we know little about the founder of Pennsylvania beyond the fact that William Penn was a flat-hat English Quaker and that he thought that *he* owned all 45,000 square miles of the territory when he made that 1683 pact with the Lenni-Lenapes.

What a story lies behind the events of that momentous day.

William Penn was the son of English Admiral Sir William Penn, a *very* influential naval officer and confidant of King Charles I (who was beheaded), Oliver Cromwell ("The Protector"), King Charles II ("The Restorer"), and indeed the entire English royal line.

With that kind of money, parental influence, educational possibilities, and superior brain power, one would expect young Penn to have enjoyed a smooth ride to the top. But it was not to be, for ever since King Henry VIII had expelled the Roman Catholic religion from England and declared the Anglican faith to be the only official state religion for all his subjects, various monarchs had been vying to enforce that decision. Suffice it to say that it was dangerous if not treasonous to profess or even discuss another denomination in England at that time.

Young William Penn, to his father's dismay, had come under the influence of a Quaker preacher and had decided at age twenty-two to declare himself publically to be a Quaker. After that time, young William was constantly a public embarrassment to his family. He was arrested and thrown into prison multiple times, and was even dismissed from Christ College, Oxford, for his support of Quakerism. Finally, his desperate father, on his deathbed, made a deal regarding his son's future with the royals.

The admiral died in 1670 and it was revealed that in order to get rid of the troublesome Quakers of England, young Penn would be given the New World property of "Pennsylvania." Well, Charles II didn't exactly *give* the land to Penn; he got the cancellation of an 18,000 pound financial debt that he owed to the late Admiral Penn. *And* young Penn was enjoined to "empty England of all these troublesome Quakers!"

In 1681 the deal was effective and thousands of Quakers (and other minorities) flocked from England and other parts of Western Europe to this New World paradise of religious equality, free elections, fair jury trials, and freedom from unjust imprisonment.

QUESTION: How did all of this turn out for the Penn family?

ANSWER: William Penn's closest financial advisor, Quaker Philip Ford, cheated Penn out of thousands of pounds and even tricked Penn into unknowingly signing a title to the Province of Pennsylvania that gave it to Ford! Penn, at age sixty-two, actually landed in debtor's prison for a time. In 1712 he suffered a series of heart attacks and strokes, but he survived for six more years as a helpless invalid. William Penn, the founder, died penniless in 1718 at age seventy-four.

Penn's family however, retained ownership of Pennsylvania right up until the American Revolution. His sons William and Thomas ("The Proprietors") ran the colony for their own benefit, renounced Quakerism, and generally undid many of their father's progressive ideas.

Molly Pitcher

It was ON THIS DAY, June 28, 1778, "one of the hottest days ever known" according to a Revolutionary War eyewitness, that Molly Pitcher was cool as a cucumber. More accurately, Molly (then known as Mary Ludwig Hays) helped the sweating, fainting, and dying soldiers to stay cool during the battle of Monmouth (New Jersey).

Did you ever wonder why on earth a young woman from Carlisle, Pennsylvania, was scurrying about on a Revolutionary War battlefield? The answer is that she was married to one John Hays, a sergeant of artillery in Washington's army. He summoned her to come and assist him with his daily living duties while serving in the Revolutionary Army.

She performed her wifely duties for several months until suddenly a huge British army under General Sir Henry Clinton appeared, marching across New Jersey on their way to New York City. Washington unhesitatingly attacked the Redcoats at Monmouth Court House and fought them to a draw.

It was during this fierce engagement that Mary Ludwig Hays found herself also in the middle of the battle. Not being a soldier, Mary took it upon herself to nurse the wounded and then to carry pitchers of cool water from a nearby stream to the overheated colonials. Soon calls of "Mary" and "Molly" and "Molly Pitcher" resounded across the shell-shocked battlefield. The name stuck and she was ever after known as Molly Pitcher.

But that's not the end of the story. Molly's husband, part of an artillery group, was struck down and lay senseless before her. Molly bravely took up the cannon ramrod and performed his military duties until the end of the battle.

It is said that her heroism came to General Washington's attention and that he made her a sergeant on the spot. In any event, both Molly and her husband John Hays survived the war and returned to live in Carlisle.

John died shortly after leaving the army and Molly wed another ex-soldier, one John McCauley. After his death, Molly applied for and received a veteran's pension for the remainder of her life.

QUESTION: What do you suppose was the amount of that pension?

ANSWER: Molly McCauley, as she was then known, survived the next ten years of her life on a pension of $40 per year! She died in Carlisle in 1832 at the age of ninety.

Joseph Smith and the Mormons

It happened ON THIS DAY, June 27, 1844, at Carthage, Missouri, when Joseph Smith and his brother Hyrum were attacked and savagely killed by an angry mob.

"Why would anyone want to murder the Smith brothers?" one might ask.

And thereby hangs a tale.

Joseph Smith was born in 1805—the fourth of ten children—into a financially hard-pressed Vermont farm family. The Smiths relocated ten times during the early years of Joseph's life, eventually ending up in the area of Palmyra, New York.

By the time that he was fifteen, Joseph Smith was ready for some divine guidance in life. There were, of course, many churches in his home area, most of the evangelistic variety. But he could not seem to choose one to join. So he prayed for divine guidance. Boy, did he get it!

One day, as he was walking in the woods, God and Jesus appeared before him. They told him not to join any church immediately but to prepare for important tasks. In 1823 he claimed that the Angel Moroni visited him and revealed the existence of some golden plates, inscribed with holy words in some unknown language. Four years later, Smith found the golden plates at a place called Hill Cumorah in New York state and managed to translate them. Then, with five other men, the immensely charismatic Joseph Smith published the *Book of Mormon* and launched the Church of Jesus Christ of Latter-Day Saints.

Smith and his followers, who called themselves Mormons, were a big success! Within fourteen years there were Mormon settlements throughout the Middle West claiming 35,000 members.

But black clouds were on the horizon. There was the slavery question. (They were against it.) There was the polygamy question. (Some were for it; some not.) There was the perceived threat of the Mormons' economic and political muscle that was just beginning to be felt.

However, when Joseph Smith declared his intention of running for president of the United States and his followers burned a newspaper-publishing house that had spoken out against Mormonism, the fuse was lighted! Smith and his brother were charged with the crime and thrown into jail.

ON THIS DAY, June 27, 1844, Joseph Smith (age thirty-nine) and his brother were forcibly removed from the jail and murdered by an angry mob.

QUESTION: What happened to the new religion after the death of its founder, Joseph Smith?

ANSWER: Brigham Young took over, leading the Mormon faithful to present-day Utah, where they prosper to this day. Eventually, some of the original followers of Joseph Smith split off, forming the Reorganized Church of Latter-Day Saints.

General George A. Custer

ON THIS DAY, June 25, 1876, excitement ran high in the United States. The Civil War was more than a decade in the past. The transcontinental railroad had connected a growing, prosperous nation. Every city, town, and village crossroad was ready to celebrate our first 100 years as a nation.

But a dark shadow hung over this happy scene, for the Indian Wars on our Northwestern frontier were far from over. The injustices foisted upon the Native Americans prior to that time continued to fester.

In any event, most of our population lived east of the Mississippi River and those nasty, marauding bands of red men were safely way "out West." The US Army, including the magnificent Seventh Cavalry led by America's most flamboyant general, George Armstrong Custer, was more than a match for "a few savages" . . . or so the US Army thought.

This, then, was the situation as the sun came up ON THIS DAY just nine days before the glorious fourth of July.

It came as a nasty shock to a nation primed for a 100th birthday celebration to suddenly hear that General Custer and every man in his Seventh Cavalry command had been wiped out!

They had been massacred by the combined forces of Chief Crazy Horse, Chief Gall, and Chief Sitting Bull leading Oglala Sioux and Cheyenne warriors at the Battle of Little Bighorn.

It was not that the Indians did not have plenty of provocation for attacking the "white devils." They did. Treaties had been broken, promises forgotten, Indian villages burned, and women, children, and old men slaughtered without warning.

81

Still, George Armstrong Custer, who had been greatly adored and greatly vilified during his lifetime, now lay dead on a Montana river bluff.

Custer had graduated from West Point, last man in the class of 1861, but just in time to bravely gallop into the melee of the American Civil War. He served the Northern cause valiantly—indeed even recklessly—as a dashing cavalry leader.

His heroics did not go unnoticed. In less than two years, just before the Battle of Gettysburg, Custer was made a brigadier general, the youngest general officer in the Union Army.

QUESTION: Just *how* young was this "boy general" at the time of his appointment?

ANSWER: George Armstrong Custer was only twenty-three years old when they pinned the brigadier's star on his tunic, and just thirty-six when he met his fate along the banks of the Little Bighorn! It happened ON THIS DAY, June 25, 1876.

A contemporary sculpture commemorates
Native Americans killed at "Custer's Last Stand."
Credit: Dave Gostisha

JULY

Airman Crashes His Way Across the English Channel

ON THIS DAY, July 25, 1909, it had been less than six years since the Wright Brothers had miraculously achieved twelve seconds of powered flight.

Now, men and women were flitting about the skies like birds, staying aloft for twenty to thirty minutes at a time!

Excitement ran high among the aspiring aeronauts of Europe in the wake of the call by the *London Daily Mail* for someone—anyone—to fly across the English Channel! The British newspaper backed up that clarion call by offering an extravagant cash prize of 1,000 British pounds (equivalent to 5,000 US dollars) to the first man or woman who would accomplish the twenty-four-mile, over-water flight.

Immediately, at least three worthy contenders were galvanized into action. All were wealthy adventurers who fancied themselves to be among the air elite. Some were well equipped with several aeroplanes each and numerous mechanics to assist them.

But let us turn our attention to the eventual winner of the prize, the one man who was his plane's designer, builder, and pilot. He was limping heavily from a previous air crash and was using crutches to make his way to the take-off point.

Our subject had spent most of his career so far inventing and manufacturing automobile headlamps. By the turn of the twentieth century he had amassed a fortune doing it. But he was not satisfied, having become consumed by his interest in aeroplanes, especially after the success of the Wright Brothers in 1903. From then until 1908 he invented, built, and crashed ten planes.

But now he had built number eleven, the "perfect" monoplane, powered by a considerably less-than-perfect engine, which tended to overheat and even stop completely in less time than it would take him to fly from Calais to Dover.

And our hero had personal problems as well . . . a nagging, weeping wife and six children. She, in fact, had made him promise *never* again to leave the ground if he should be successful in flying the Channel.

So, On This Day, July 25, 1909, he got up at 4 a.m. and revved up the little monoplane for a trial run before the missus and kids could stop him.

By 4:40 a.m. the sun was also up, the motor was purring nicely, and a light breeze was blowing in from the southwest. He gassed up, strapped his crutches to the fuselage, and took off for the White Cliffs of Dover!

True to form, the engine began to overheat, but a fortuitous rain shower cooled it sufficiently to allow him to complete the flight.

And complete it he did! Thirty-seven minutes after leaving France, the dirty, oily, little boxwood and wire monoplane, and its equally dirty and oily pilot, crash-landed in the English countryside. He had won the *Daily Mail*'s prize!

QUESTION: Who was that intrepid Frenchman who, just five years before the start of World War I, first flew the Channel On This Day?

ANSWER: Louis Bleriot was his name. His wife eventually forgave him and agreed to allow him to continue his aeronautical career for the rest of his days. Bleriot passed away in 1936, but it was not as a result of an airplane crash.

P.S. The plane still is in existence. It's on display in a Paris museum, where you may see it.

Ice Cream Cone: Can't be Beat, But *Can* be Licked

Ah yes, the lazy, hazy days of summer. This weather brings to mind visions of picnics with watermelon and big, drippy ice cream cones—especially the latter, for I love even the thought of ice cream!

Really, I am nuts about ice cream. So was the Emperor Nero. Of course, *he* was nuts, period! But I digress.

July is National Ice Cream Month and ON THIS DAY, July 23, 1904, some people say that the ice cream cone was invented.

There is no doubt that a lot of ice cream was sold ON THIS DAY at The Louisiana Purchase Exposition in St. Louis, Missouri, just 100 years after Lewis and Clark had set off to explore the new territory so recently purchased from France and added to the United States. As many as fifty ice cream vendors were working the big fair and no doubt they all had some version of a walk-around ice cream container.

However, it is worth noting that a US patent had been issued on December 15, 1903, to one Italo Marciony, an ice cream pushcart purveyor from New York City, upon his invention of the ice cream cone! If my math skills are still working, that is more than six months before our ON THIS DAY date of July 23, 1904.

Earlier, I mentioned nutty old Nero. He had slaves run to the mountains to scoop up containers of snow and then run back to Rome with the essential part of his frozen dinnertime treat. And woe be unto the runner who arrived at the palace with only a bucket of ice water! This was the first century AD, of course.

Ancient Chinese apparently enjoyed an ice-cream-like dessert (probably more like sorbet), and they in turn inspired Marco Polo, who introduced it to Europe in the late thirteenth century AD.

All of these early concoctions were nondairy treats. The first dairy delight that we know of was consumed by King Charles I of England and his guests in the 1640s. They (rebels, not his guests) cut his head off in 1649, so we don't really know if he liked the ice cream or not. In any event, his chefs sold the recipe to the nobility of Europe and we were off and dripping.

The idea leaped the Atlantic in the early 1700s, and we know that George Washington, Thomas Jefferson, and Dolley Madison (wife of President James) served it on special occasions.

Still, it was real work to make ice cream until 1847, when a smart young woman named Nancy Johnson developed and patented the hand-cranked ice cream freezer.

Which brings us to the twentieth century, when advances in refrigeration and power usage allowed for mass production of the tasty treat. However ON THIS DAY in 1904 the US still produced less than ten million gallons of ice cream each year.

QUESTION: How many gallons of that delicious dessert do you suppose we manufacture today?

ANSWER: Over 1 *billion* gallons every year! Time now to cool off and visit your favorite ice cream shop. See you there.

Credit: Becco Eliacik

Benjamin Franklin: "Early to bed and early to rise . . ."

Just three months after the beginning of the American Revolution, ON THIS DAY, July 26, 1775, Benjamin Franklin was named by the Continental Congress to be our first postmaster general. He was eminently qualified for the job.

Thirty-eight years before his Colonial postmastership, in 1737, Franklin had been appointed postmaster of Philadelphia. At that time he was also the publisher of his newspaper, the *Pennsylvania Gazette*, and the two occupations seemed to mesh rather well. As postmaster of Philadelphia, Franklin was able to increase the circulation of his paper via the city's postal service. Through his efforts, mail delivery times were cut almost in half.

Moving right along to 1753, Benjamin Franklin was made joint postmaster general of the colonies by the British Crown. In this position, the ever-enthusiastic Franklin made a tour of the major post offices in *all* cities of the American colonies.

Franklin served as interim postmaster general for the Crown for twenty-two years, making necessary improvements such as standardizing postal routes, establishing postal roads from Maine to Florida, instituting a system of auditing post offices, and presumably still finding time to pursue all of his many other interests. He was dismissed by the British in 1774 because of his outspoken support for the cause of independence for the Colonies. But not to worry, a new postmaster job was waiting in the wings for the Pennsylvanian.

Which brings us to THIS DAY, July 26, 1775, when Benjamin Franklin went to work heading up the Postal Service for the united colonies. They needed a smoothly functioning mail system right away, and he gave them just that.

Franklin soon had Colonial mail service from Portland, Maine, to Savannah, Georgia. He even gave his postmaster salary back to the government for the relief of wounded Revolutionary soldiers! What a man!

I am a great admirer of Benjamin Franklin—statesman, scientist, public leader, postmaster, and the *only* man to sign all four of the most important treaties and documents of the Revolutionary War period.

QUESTION: Do you know which they were?

ANSWER: Franklin put his pen to the Declaration of Independence, the Treaty of Alliance with France, the Treaty to end the Revolutionary War, and the US Constitution.

Johann Sebastian Bach: Man of Notes Born

ON THIS DAY, July 28, 1750, at age sixty-five, the musical genius of Johann Sebastian Bach was snuffed out. He had been losing his eyesight during the last year of his life and his condition was worsened by two unsuccessful cataract operations, aggravated by an infection that finally caused his death.

During those last months, J.S. Bach continued working, still composing in a darkened room because the light hurt his eyes. His musical thoughts were put on paper by the hand of his son-in-law but they were surely Bach's own. Appropriately, his last completed work was entitled "Before Thy Throne O Lord, I Stand"!

One more amazing event occurred on the day that he died. He woke up that morning to find that he could see quite clearly! It only lasted for several hours, but it bordered on the miraculous.

Johann Sebastian Bach was born on March 21, 1685, into a musical family in the strongly Lutheran central German province of Thuringia. "Musical family" puts his connections mildly for no fewer than forty-two of his relatives were professional musicians of varying kinds and achievements. His father was the court trumpeter and director of musicians for the Duke of Eisenach, and Dad lost no time in indoctrinating young Johann into the intricacies of music; teaching him to play the violin, the harpsichord, and the organ before his eighth birthday. At that time, Johann discovered that he also possessed a fine soprano voice and that he enjoyed choral music.

Tragically, before he was nine years old, Johann lost a sister and a brother to disease; then his mother died, to be followed nine months later by his father! As a result, Bach was transplanted into the home of an older brother, who just happened to be the church organist in the village of Ohrdruf. Through him, J.S. learned all of the mysteries of both the organ and the harpsichord and also began the study of musical composition. And, if that were not enough, young Bach just happened to be on hand when the new church organ was installed in the Ohrdruf Church. The mechanics of organ building and repair became another Bach passion.

Suffice it to say, by the time he was eighteen years of age, Johann Sebastian Bach had mastered the tools of his profession. He spent the remainder of his life working for various electors, dukes, princes, and other royals of the many principalities making up the German state.

During his lifetime, Bach was mostly known as an organist and an expert in organ construction, but he also composed a profusion of beautiful secular and religious music that did not really gain popularity until after his death.

It was his good fortune to be born at the right time and place possessing transcendent compositional talents. He helped raise High Baroque music to its very heights and when he died ON THIS DAY, it began a gradual decline.

J.S. Bach produced three great church works, over 300 church cantatas, many secular cantatas, six major orchestral works, plus countless fugues, fantasias, passacaglias, and a bunch of little Bachs.

QUESTION: How many little musicians were forthcoming?

ANSWER: Bach and his two wives managed to pass on their musical genes to twenty children!

The Potato: Tubers are Terrific

Happy birthday to you. Happy birthday to you. Happy birthday dear tuber, Happy birthday to you!

Well, it's not *exactly* the birthday of the potato, but as far as we know, July 28, 1586, marks the introduction by a famous English nobleman of the white potato into England and Ireland. And thereby hangs a tale.

Now, if the potato was unknown on the continent of Europe until the late 1500s, where do you suppose this nutritious, hearty, easy-to-grow food had been hiding? The story has its roots some 7,000 years ago in the wind-swept frigid Andes mountains of South America, where the durable tuber happily grew undisturbed at elevations up to 15,000 feet, regardless of climatic and soil conditions.

Then came 1492, and Columbus and Balboa and Cortez and Pizarro and the Spanish *conquistadores* who followed them. I'm not saying that the Spanish soldiers were mad with joy when they first came across the potato plant growing in the upper reaches of present-day Peru and Bolivia, but since they stole everything else from the South American Indians, they also took the potato plant with them when they sailed home.

This brings us to the 1570s, when the potato was cultivated for the next 200 years in Europe not as a food, but as a botanical curiosity by amateur scientists. The tuber was, after all, a member of the nightshade family, and its leaves are poisonous to humans, if eaten.

Now we swing back to July 28, 1586, when the aforementioned English nobleman decided to plant a few potatoes on his Irish estate. "What the heck," he thought, "I can always feed them to the animals." To his surprise, the potato grew well in the rocky soil and temperate climate of Ireland.

Eventually the common people began growing potatoes in their back yards and actually eating them. Soon English settlers took the potato plant with them as they embarked for the New World.

So for the next 250 years the world chomped away on the potato, making it a staple part of its diet. Then in 1845 a two-year disaster struck Ireland in the form of potato blight, and thousands of Irish people died of starvation. Many of the survivors immigrated to the United States to escape the potato famine, only to find that the peripatetic potato had preceded them here by several hundred years.

So what goes around comes around. What began 7,000 years ago in the high Andes of South America is now adorning your dinner plate as french fries.

QUESTION: Who was that famous English nobleman who first introduced the potato on his Irish plantation and then sent it on its way to North America?

ANSWER: It was Sir Walter Raleigh, a favorite of Queen Elizabeth I. He later fell out of favor with her successors, who ordered his head cut off. But that's another story!

Credit: Jonathan Ruchti

AUGUST

Pompeii: Big Blow Up
in the "Boot"

Location, location, location. It was the same in ancient Pompeii ON THIS DAY in 79 AD as it is in the world of today. Location was everything. Everyone who could afford it wanted to live in that lovely seaside town. Oh, there had been earthquakes now and again, plus warnings that towering Mt. Vesuvius could erupt again, but Pompeii was such a wonderful place to live—quite unlike crowded, filthy, nearby Naples.

Everyone knows what comes next, but mostly we have after-the-fact versions of the catastrophe. What say that we go ON THIS DAY to an eyewitness account, directly translated from the Latin writings of Pliny the Younger as reported by the Roman historian Tacitus, describing the happenings of August 24, 79 AD.

To set the stage, there were three Plinys there: "the Younger," his uncle "The Elder," and the mother of "the Younger." They were about twelve miles from Mt. Vesuvius on the day before the eruptions started. The earth had been trembling for several days, and occasionally loud rumbles came from the mountain. This had happened before, but the populace had failed to pay much attention. As a matter of fact, repair work on buildings damaged by earlier eruptions had already been started, and life proceeded as usual in Pompeii.

Then about one p.m. on August 23, a large white cloud erupted from the cone of Vesuvius. At about that same time, a messenger arrived at the Plinys' location, bringing the first news of widespread panic and of residents fleeing their homes.

At this point, Pliny the Elder was galvanized into action. He had a close friend in Pompeii whom he determined to save. Setting out in a sailboat with the wind at his back, Pliny the Elder quickly arrived at Pompeii's port. He soon found that he could not land because of floating pumice in the waters adjacent to the city. Sailing on quickly to the next town of Stabie, Pliny the Elder finally located his friend. But alas, once he had landed he found that the earthquake had so changed the formation of the gulf that he could not escape! And the wind had changed direction. Thus both men were trapped and eventually perished in the rain of fire, stone, and molten lava that was soon to pour from the top of an angry mountain!

Meanwhile, Pliny the Younger and his mother sat on that hilltop twelve miles away, where they witnessed another white cloud erupting. This one looked like a pine tree, Pliny said. They watched it expand, flatten out, become darker and much closer the ground. Pyrotechnics continued all night on the 23rd and well into the next morning.

By this time the Plinys had seen enough. Early on the morning of the 24th, they fled from the holocaust, running toward higher ground through hot ashes, darkness, and poisonous fumes. Carts rolled back and forth as the earth heaved! The sea retreated from the wind, only to return as a lethal tsunami wave. Then came the horrible black clouds and winds containing long tongues of fire propelled by strong explosions. It was as if it was a pitch-black night engulfed everything. And it was hard to breathe, even from more than twelve miles away.

By afternoon, thirteen *feet* of pumice covered the ground of Pompeii. Animals and people alike were unable to walk or run through it. Then came the molten lava, totally destroying any buildings still sticking up through the ash. More than 2,000 residents who had decided to "stick it out" perished that day. The ashes from the eruption were carried by the wind as far away as Egypt, Libya, and Syria. Widespread disease went with them.

When the ash settled and the lava hardened, Pompeii was effectively sealed like an ancient time capsule. This all happened ON THIS DAY, August 24, 79 AD.

QUESTION: How long do you suppose it took until professional large-scale excavations of the buried city began?

ANSWER: They finally got around to begin digging it out after nearly 1,700 years had passed! But believe me, it was worth the wait. I've seen it and you should, too.

The Liberation of Paris: The City of Light Relit

ON THIS DAY, August 25, 1944, the whole world cheered wildly as the mostly undamaged city of Paris was liberated from the grip of the Nazis and their French collaborationists. Well, not *everyone* was wildly happy.

Adolph Hitler was insanely *un*happy that Paris had not been blown up and burned according to his orders! He was also understandably upset that his troops had surrendered or fled without putting up much of a fight.

General Dwight Eisenhower, the Allies' Supreme Commander, was steaming mad that the Free French forces commanded by General Charles DeGaulle had disobeyed his orders to wait for the bulk of the US Second Armored Division before forcing entry into the city.

Meanwhile, the French Resistance fighters already in the city had stirred up a hornet's nest with overt acts of violence against the German occupiers and collaborationists as soon as they heard that Allied troops were approaching the city gates. This too was against their standing orders from General "Ike."

Ever since June 1940, France had been under the firm control of Nazi Germany. They had militarily occupied the northern and western parts of France and had set up a collaborationist regime for the rest of France, headquartered in the central French city of Vichy. Now, more than four years later, the Allies had successfully landed massive army groups at Normandy, and the "breakout" race for open ground was underway. It looked as if the end was at hand for the Nazi occupiers of the City of Light.

General Ike Eisenhower, supreme commander of the Allied invasion forces, had not originally planned to liberate Paris quite so soon. The American and British forces were intent on destroying the Nazi armies, who were then retreating towards the Rhine. Actually, Eisenhower's battle plan was to beat the Russians to the capture of Berlin and thus quickly end the war. As I'm sure you know, things didn't quite work out that way in late August of 1944.

Eisenhower's hand was forced by the actions of Free French Generals DeGaulle and LeClerc, who on the eve of August 24, notified Supreme Headquarters that the next day they would "take" Paris, ignoring Ike's orders to wait for stronger back up. Finally the US Second Armored Division and the US Fourth Infantry Division were rushed to the front to participate in the Liberation of Paris with the Free French forces, entering the city ON THIS DAY, August 25, 1944.

Meanwhile, German General Dietrich von Choltiz, who was the military governor of Paris and of whom it was said that—despite some despicable wartime actions previously committed—he was now leaning toward saving the cultural treasures of the French capital from senseless destruction. No doubt he also was aware that, had he allowed the destruction to occur, he might have been branded a war criminal. In any event, he knew that the war was coming to an end and he didn't care to risk being a last-minute casualty. Under his orders, and in defiance of Hitler's edict, Paris was left mostly intact and the German garrison just "melted away," running for all they were worth toward Germany or quickly surrendering to the oncoming forces. Oh yes, there was considerable backstage bargaining between von Choltiz and undercover Allied agents to allow for the "Miracle of Paris" to happen! But that is another whole story.

And now to the towering Free French General Charles DeGaulle. He was the unelected but designated (by himself and his supporters) president of the provisional government of the French Republic, but he was nonetheless not recognized by all as the legitimate head of the government of France. It took three months of additional political wrangling among the Allied governments to finally have DeGaulle made "official." The new national unity government was politically divided (to say the least), containing anarchists, communists, Gaullists, and nationalists!

Wow! And you thought the Normandy landings were tough on poor old General Ike! Arranging for the capture of an undefended Paris proved to be nearly as difficult.

However, there was a high price to pay for the "easy" liberation of Paris. The war was unnecessarily extended by more than eight months and thousands of combatants were killed in the subsequent fighting that bought Paris its freedom.

QUESTION: When did Germany finally surrender and the war in Europe come to an end?

ANSWER: May 7, 1945, was the day when Germany finally capitulated to the Allies, thus closing the bloody pages of World War II in Europe.

Edwin Drake Discovers Oil: Ten Cents a Barrel

I'll bet that not many of you even know where Titusville, Pennsylvania, is, let alone what world-changing event happened there. Well, it was On This Day, August 27, 1859, near the small northwestern Pennsylvania town of Titusville, when one Edwin L. Drake and his good friend and local blacksmith, "Uncle Billy" Smith, drilled the first commercially successful producing oil well in the United States!

Some of the useful properties of oil had been known for thousands of years: The ancient Egyptians, the Babylonians, the Chinese, and our own North American Indians appreciated petroleum's healing and lubricating properties.

Before 1859 oil had only been recovered in buckets when it seeped naturally from the earth, or at best from hand-dug shallow wells, but going deeper for oil—that was another matter. Various groups had been going broke for years in northwestern Pennsylvania, sinking unproductive, deep wells that usually failed because of cave-ins and flooding.

But On This Day, E.L. Drake had a better idea! He used a steel pipe casing to prevent collapse or water problems, driving the casing down to solid rock at sixty-nine feet. Still no oil came up. Not to worry. Old E.L. and Uncle Billy had another idea. Why not drill *through* the rock?

A steam-operated mechanical drill was hired. Six more inches were driven through the rock. And viola! There was *oil*! To be honest with you, it wasn't exactly a gusher; in fact the oil barely came up to the top of the casing. However, a small pneumatic pump quickly took care of that problem.

Thirty-five barrels per day of black gold began bubbling out! At $20 per barrel, that amounted to a tidy daily gross for two old guys, even in 1859.

The newly anointed oil barons were so proud of their accomplishment that they told everyone how they did it! And then, of course, soon everyone around Titusville, Pennsylvania, was drilling for oil, thus driving the price down to *ten cents* per barrel by 1862! In a short time the Commonwealth was awash in oil. It was being shipped out by wagon, rail, and boat, by a brand-new five-mile pipeline.

As you may have guessed, Edwin L. Drake did not start out in life as a petroleum engineer.

QUESTION: What was his original occupation?

ANSWER: "Colonel" Drake, as he was later known, was a retired railroad conductor, a handyman whose latent abilities gave him a chance at a second career—and a place in history—beginning ON THIS DAY, August 27, 1859. Too bad the old boy couldn't have waited another 150 years for the discovery of oil. It's been worth up to $120 per barrel within the past several years!

Mohammad Reza Shah Pahlavi was
emperor of Iran from 1949 to 1979.
Credit: Ghazarians

Iran Sheds the Shah

ON THIS DAY, August 22, 1953, the Shah of Iran returned to power. Actually, he hadn't been gone too long. As a matter of fact, he and his royal entourage had been partying in exile in Baghdad for only a few weeks when the call came that the combined efforts of the US CIA, British MI-5, and Israeli Mossad Secret Service organizations had overthrown Iranian Prime Minister Mohammad Mossdegh and that the Shah could safely return to Teheran.

Ah yes, the Shah. I had almost forgotten about him and, except for *oil*, I suspect that much of the rest of the world would also have put him out of its collective mind.

Mohammad Reza Pahlavi had been installed on the "peacock throne" during World War II by a British-Russian invasion that forced his neutralist father to abdicate in favor of his pro-western son. Again, it was *oil* that precipitated the move. Shortly after taking power, the Shah's new government and the Anglo-Iranian Oil Company took control of the vast Iranian petroleum fields, nationalizing them "in the name of the people."

He was a handsome man; his life was a real throwback to the Arabian Nights. Though of humble birth, in later years the Pahlavis even suggested they descended from Cyrus the Great and a 2,500-year old Persian royal line! He was known as His Imperial Majesty, Shahinshah, the King of Kings, a Light unto the Aryans. The Shah lived a grand life housed in an imperial palace, served by courtiers who followed him everywhere and dressed in gold-encrusted military uniforms hung with pounds of glittering medals. He was married to three gorgeous Muslim women (one at a time) in pursuit of a suitable male heir. He rode, he danced, he flew, and he traveled the world. He was the very model of a modern Western-supported monarch. And it was all in the name of *oil*.

In fairness, it must be said that the Shah also tried to serve the interests of the Iranian people while steadily westernizing his nation, but to a large extent he failed them. His rule became more and more autocratic, and in the end the Shah was overthrown in 1979 by Iranian forces led by his own disaffected Muslim Shi'a clergy, forcing him to flee the country again.

Sadly, he shortly discovered that he had cancer and he became a "homeless" wanderer among Western medical-treatment centers. Eventually, Mohammad Reza Pahlavi, the deposed Shah of Iran, succumbed to the disease, dying on July 27, 1980.

QUESTION: Do you know where he is buried?

ANSWER: He lies in Cairo, Egypt, in the Al Rifa mosque alongside his onetime brother in law, King Farouk of Egypt. Empress Farah Diba lives on in exile, as does Crown Prince Reza Pahlavi.

SEPTEMBER

William the Conqueror
Earns His Nickname

Today is the anniversary of the beginning of the Norman Conquest, the last time a successful invasion of England took place.

An armada of 600 ships and 7,000 men landed in County Sussex ON THIS DAY, September 28, 1066, led by a fighting mad William, Duke of Normandy.

It's no wonder he was angry, for according to William—a grand-nephew of the English king—he had been promised the English throne some thirteen years before by the then-monarch, Edward the Confessor. However, in January of 1066, Edward died and one Harold Godwinson was selected by the English authorities to be king.

Wasting no time, Godwinson was duly crowned as King Harold II of England on January 5, 1066, because he claimed that the dying Edward the Confessor, who was his brother-in-law, had named him (Harold) as the heir *and* also because Harold's family controlled four of the strongest and largest counties in the south of England!

The matter was further complicated by William's story that Harold, who in 1064 had been shipwrecked off the coast of Normandy and briefly held prisoner, had at that time sworn "on the holy bones of several saints" that he (Harold) would support William's claim to the English throne when the time came.

But when Edward died, Harold took the throne for himself, and so the fateful year of 1066 dawned with a new king on the throne of England and an understandably outraged William ready to sail from France to claim his "rightful place" as the king of England.

Now, stay with me. It gets even more exciting!

Although he was now the English sovereign, Harold II was not yet out of the woods, so to speak. King Harold was continually harassed by three of his brothers, who had become the powerful earls of a large part of northern England. But his biggest threat came from—would you believe—Norway, via King Harald Hardrada, who also claimed the right to the English throne.

Hardrada had sailed his Viking longboats to the northern shores of England and had promptly defeated the defenders. This forced King Harold II to move his forces north rapidly, thereby exposing his southern flank to William's invasion fleet. Well, Harold defeated and killed Hardrada, whose men then promptly sailed home. But it was too late! For William had already landed in Sussex and soundly defeated King Harold's tired and disorganized troops. England's King Harold was killed in the battle, and William of Normandy became "William the Conqueror."

QUESTION: What is the name of that famous battle that earned William the Conqueror the right to the English throne?

ANSWER: It is still known as the Battle of Hastings, won by William the Conqueror, who then was promptly crowned in London's Westminster Abbey on Christmas Day, 1066 as William the First of England.

Nathan Hale: He Tried, But Failed

The revolution had hardly begun when suddenly it was over—forever—for a mild-mannered former schoolteacher from Connecticut ON THIS DAY, September 22, 1776.

The opening year of the revolt against His Majesty King George III's red-coated soldiers had not been an easy one for the colonists. Of course there was the exhilaration of Lexington and Concord in 1775, but those had been small moving skirmishes that no one really won. Then came the Battle of Bunker Hill, which everyone thinks the Americans won. Actually, the British were victorious in their third charge up the hill, sweeping the rag-tag Colonial army from the heights.

The final action late in the year saw the patriots, under the leadership of Generals Benedict Arnold and Richard Montgomery, invading Canada, almost but not quite capturing both Montreal and Quebec. However, 10,000 fresh British troops were rushed up the St. Lawrence to the defense of Quebec and that was that.

Things took a turn for the better in March of 1776, with George Washington's fortification of Dorchester Heights overlooking Boston, showing the British the wisdom of evacuating the city. They did, promptly sailing off to occupy the New York area. Wow! Now the Americans were really in a pickle!

General Washington had placed about one third of his forces on Long Island, hoping to blunt the powerful redcoat force that faced him. But he was foiled again by a surprise attack on August 27, 1776, by General Sir William Howe's Regulars, who forced the Colonials back to Manhattan.

By now the American commander-in-chief was getting desperate. He needed information about the disposition of those British troops who were preparing to winter in little old New York. What to do? There was no CIA, FBI, Secret Service, or anything like that to come to Washington's rescue. So what *did* he do? Well he asked for volunteers of course. No one responded. A second call for volunteers went out.

The Americans needed just one man to go behind the British lines to secure the needed military information. This time a small "I'll go" came from an unlikely source—Captain Nathan Hale, a quiet, pious, former schoolteacher, a graduate of Yale University, who had just turned twenty-one.

So he went, in civilian clothes, trying to pass himself off as a Dutch schoolmaster. He did it successfully, getting all the necessary information concerning troops, supplies, and placements that General Washington so badly needed. But alas, on the way home he was betrayed (some say by his cousin, an ardent Royalist), caught with the goods on him, and sentenced to hang for treason on the following day, September 22, 1776.

QUESTION: What were Nathan Hale's last words?

ANSWER: We don't know. Really, we don't. The "I only regret that I have but one life to lose for my country" is just a tradition, probably made up by Washington to inspire the troops. Heaven knows that they would need a lot of inspiration to get through the next seven years.

Nathan Hale was hanged as a spy.
Credit: UShistoryimages.com/Lossing

George Stephenson: Inventor
Works up a Full Head of Steam

He was a kind of a British Thomas Edison, and—like that US genius—George Stephenson frequently turned his agile mind to many of the day's most vexing problems.

But his most important work, the development of an efficiently working steam locomotive, culminated ON THIS DAY, September 27, 1825. It took place on iron-topped wooden rails running between the towns of Durham and Darlington in the sparsely populated Northumberland/Durham area of northern England.

A large, cheering crowd gathered to see George Stephenson climb aboard and take the controls of the *Locomotion* as it began its maiden journey by pulling thirty-six wagons behind it! All of the cheering people were, however, standing beside the slowly moving engine. None was riding in any of the wagons being pulled. That would come later. They were now filled with sacks of coal and flour.

Let me hasten to point out that George Stephenson did not *invent* the steam engine; nor did James Watt, who is often credited with doing so. This honor goes to a little-known Englishman named Thomas Savery, way back in 1698.

Many Englishmen were working diligently on the problems of steam locomotion in the 127 years from Savery to Stephenson. For they knew there was a real need for more efficient motive power. This was, after all, the era of the Industrial Revolution in England. Coal mining and the production of wrought iron cried out for help from inventors.

George Stephenson had been born into this milieu. His father worked in a colliery and his place of birth was right beside a horse-drawn wagonway from the mines. As a boy, George had herded cows instead of going to school and had gone to work in the mines at fourteen. But he proved to be an ambitious boy, deciding to attend night school at eighteen and finally learn to read and write!

His contributions to steam locomotion went beyond just improving the locomotive. George had also figured out that wooden rails topped with iron would make a much better roadway. He also came up with the engineering idea that an absolutely flat roadbed would provide a much better rolling surface. All this eventually led to research on and the building of tunnels, bridges, viaducts, and speedier and more efficient engines.

But I digress. ON THIS DAY, September 27, 1825, George Stephenson was demonstrating his newest achievement. The *Locomotion* worked perfectly over the nine miles of track from Durham to Darlington.

QUESTION: How long do you suppose it took to reach his destination?

ANSWER: Only two hours. Some parts of the journey saw it reach the then-terrifying speed of fifteen miles per hour! It happened ON THIS DAY, only twelve years before a similar, though improved, steam locomotive and iron rails reached Chambersburg, Pennsylvania, for the very first time!

Caesar Augustus: Octavian Becomes the New Caesar

Well, you probably haven't thought much about him recently, but today is Caesar Augustus' birthday. If the old boy had just hung on a bit longer and if we were still using the Julian calendar, he would be more than 2,073 years old! Not bad even for a godly figure such as he had imagined himself.

Born ON THIS DAY, September 23, 63 BC, Octavian, as he was originally known, was Julius Caesar's grandnephew. As it turned out, Octavian was also the apple of his eye!

As we all know, Julius Caesar was assassinated on the Ides of March, 44 BC, when Octavian was just nineteen years of age. The entire Roman world was electrified by the news of Caesar's murder and by the equally big news that the young Octavian had been adopted by Caesar and made his royal heir under the terms of Caesar's will!

But the lucky young heir soon discovered that Marc Antony, Caesar's former chief adviser, was in firm control of Rome and not at all willing to share anything with Octavian. So young Octavian, leading an army of Caesar's veteran soldiers, challenged, met, and defeated Antony on the field of battle within the year. Now more amenable to a compromise, Marc Antony, Octavian, and a Roman general named Lepidus formed a triumvirate to rule Rome with an iron fist. In 40 BC, Antony decided to consolidate his power and to extend it by marrying Octavian's sister, Octavia!

Now bear with me here, gentle readers, for this story reads like a script for "Real Housewives of the Roman World." The Triumvirate (mostly Octavian and Antony) killed more than 2,000 of their enemies, including Grand Uncle

Julius' assassins, the great orator Cicero, and Pompey the Younger, and then had General Lepidus exiled and removed from power!

Then Antony made his big mistakes: casting aside his well-connected wife, marrying Cleopatra (yes, *that* Cleopatra), moving to Egypt, producing heirs with her, and giving the kids Roman provinces as birthday presents!

An infuriated Octavian sent his best General/Admiral Marcus Agrippa to end this nonsense. And end it he did—decisively—in 31 BC, at the naval battle of Actium off the west coast of Greece, where he defeated the combined fleets of Cleopatra and Antony. Within the year, both Queen Cleopatra and Marc Antony had committed suicide.

Now Octavian was in supreme power in Rome. By 27 BC he had forced the Roman Senate to grant him the powers of "dictator for life"—award him the name Caesar Augustus—and to make him finally the first Roman emperor.

Surprisingly, he did very well during his forty-one-year rule, restoring peace and order, honest government, a sound currency, free trade with the other Roman provinces, an efficient postal system, and improved roads and harbors. What's not to like?

But great as he was, Caesar Augustus will be forever remembered for a routine order he put out mandating that a census be taken of all persons living in the Roman Empire in 4 BC.

QUESTION: What was the enduring effect of this census order?

ANSWER: You'll find the answer in the *Bible*, Luke 2, 1-7 (Revised Standard Version). "In those days a decree went out from Caesar Augustus that all the world would . . ."

And so it came to pass, as prophesied, that Jesus Christ would be born in Bethlehem, the city of David, where his parents had gone to be counted in the Roman census.

OCTOBER

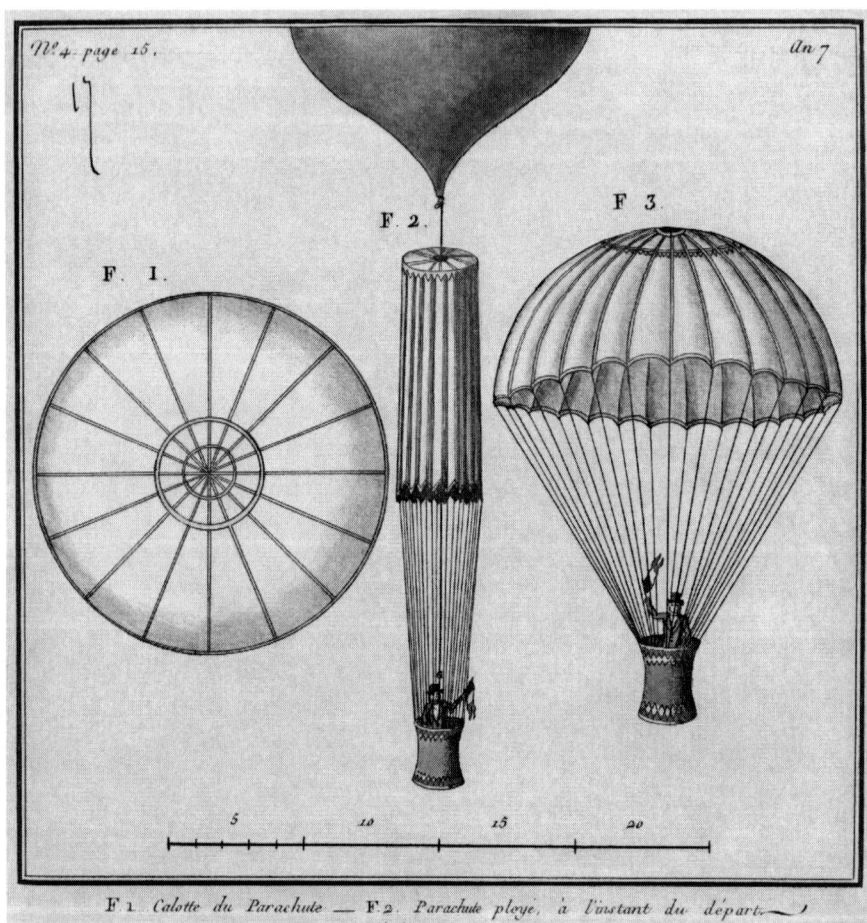

F. 1.   Calotte du Parachute ___ F. 2. Parachute ploye, à l'instant du départ.___ ✓
F. 3 ... Parachute déploye, à l'instant de la séparation d'avec le ballon.

Andre Jacques Garnerin made world's first parachute jump, shown in these illustrations (left to right): the parachute canopy seen from above; the parachute rises into the air; the parachute separates from the balloon.

World's First Parachute Jump:
That First Step is a Big One

I've always been a nut for stories about airplanes. As you probably know, we recently marked the 100th anniversary of the Wright Brothers' invention of the first heavier-than-air, man-carrying, powered aircraft.

While this story is about flying, it is not about airplanes. At times we forget that there are other ways to propel oneself through the air. For example, there's the lighter-than-air balloon—filled with hot air or hydrogen or helium in versions that may be powered, tethered, or free-floating. All of which brings us to an event that occurred in Paris more than 200 years ago, ON THIS DAY, October 22, 1797.

Those "crazee" Frenchmen, the Montgolfier brothers, and their many imitators had been crisscrossing the skies above Paris for some fourteen years. In 1785 two intrepid aeronauts had actually crossed the English Channel (Dover to Calais) in a lighter-than-air balloon equipped with oar-like devices to help steer it through the air! Soon it seemed everyone was flying. There were balloon demonstrations in England, France, Italy, and Austria. No one wanted to be left behind.

But I digress. By 1797, the balloon had even been used in a few skirmishes of the French Revolution, and the first fatality from a suddenly falling balloon had already occurred. Somebody needed to invent an emergency escape device, and somebody had. Believe it or not, the parachute had already been invented (or at least sketched out) more than 300 years before that first balloon flight!

Anyway, ON THIS DAY, using those ancient drawings to construct a homemade parachute, another "crazee" Frenchman named Andre Jacques Garnerin made the world's first parachute jump. He leaped from the basket of a balloon, soaring along some 3,000 feet over Paris, and lived to tell the tale. We don't know if the jump was just an experiment or if it was a forced departure from the balloon. We do, however, know that the parachute that he used was barely eight feet in diameter!

Question: Who knows the name of the genius that invented the parachute 300 years before it was needed?

Answer: Of course, who else but the genius of the Renaissance, Leonardo da Vinci, who also had foreseen manned flight, leaving us 150 sketches of "flapping wing" devices and even one of a helicopter. Leonardo's labors finally bore fruit On This Day, October 22, 1797, when his sketches made possible the first successful parachute jump.

WSM Radio and The Grand Ole Opry: Barn Dance a Big Hit

The year 1925 was a big one for the radio broadcasting business in the United States. Only five years before, the very first commercial AM station had debuted in Pittsburgh. But by the mid-1920s there were a half dozen "clear channel" stations emanating from many of America's larger cities. Now it was Nashville's turn to shine.

On October 5, 1925, WSM signed on for its very first day of broadcasting. One thousand "hot watts" pushed out voice and music from 650 KCS on the radio dial, day and night.

After a month of aimless programming, the newly hired Program Director George D. Hay, who styled himself as "the solemn old judge," decided that they would have themselves some good old country music, a "barn dance," as he called it.

Since all radio was "live" radio in those days, Hay had his work cut out for him. He knew that the Tennessee hills abounded with home-grown fiddle and banjo players, down-home singers, and comic characters of every kind. All he had to do was find them.

And find them he did. On, November 28, 1925, The WSM Barn Dance officially hit the airwaves. Its first star was Uncle Jimmy Thompson, a seventy-seven-year-old mule driver and country fiddler who bragged that he could "fiddle the bugs off'n a tater vine!"

Uncle Jimmy was an immediate hit with the listeners, and he was soon followed by the likes of Dr. Humphrey Bates and the Possum Hunters; DeFord Bailey, the Harmonica Wizard; The Fruit Jar Drinkers; The Crook

Brothers; The Gully Jumpers; and a beloved banjo player called Uncle Dave Macon. What a crew!

The telegrams with requests poured in. The Barn Dance moved from small studio to large studio to a theatre to a tabernacle to the War Memorial Auditorium to Ryman Auditorium, and finally to its present home in the 4,000-seat Grand Ole Opry House.

Early on, radio station WSM—Nashville became an affiliate of the National Broadcasting Company. The Barn Dance further enhanced its growing audience on the NBC network every Saturday at 10 p.m. It was still called The Barn Dance until December of 1927, when it got its now famous moniker "The Grand Ole Opry."

QUESTION: Would you by any chance know how this new name came to be?

ANSWER: Back in 1927, The Barn Dance was preceded by Dr. Walter Damrosch and the NBC Symphony Orchestra. On that fateful December evening, no doubt tired of listening to hours of classical music, The solemn old judge, announcer George Hay, began The Barn Dance by saying, "You have been listening to music from grand opera. Now we are going to hear some tunes from The Grand Ole Opry." And the name just refused to go away.

Pablo Picasso: Cubism Arrives Big Time

Pablo Picasso, one of the twentieth century's greatest artists, was born ON THIS DAY, October 25, 1881. He was Spanish by birth, and my late wife and I just happened to be in the Prado Museum in Madrid on the day of his death. We were literally surrounded by Picasso's artworks—items from his Blue Period, his Rose Period, and by many examples from his long-lived Cubist Period.

Everyone in the Prado became instantly silent at the announcement of his passing. Then came the weeping . . . the wailing . . . the moaning . . . the cries of misery at the thought that there would be no new Picasso art in the world.

Personally, I was glad to think that and I felt like cheering and yelling "Yay, no more of those awful Picasso paintings!" I didn't, of course, but I really do hate his work. If you would like to personally check him out, try the nearest art book, or go to MOMA in New York City or the National Gallery in Washington.

He came into this world a child prodigy, and he was pushed along the art trail at a very early age by his art-teacher father. He soon graduated to the bars of Barcelona and then, as a rebellious teenager, moved back and forth between Spain and Paris for the next five years, finally settling in Paris in the early years of the twentieth century.

He already knew how to paint pretty pictures better than most of his contemporaries, but he wanted something more. He was intent on soaking up the last morsels of art knowledge from the styles of such French masters as Manet, Courbet, and especially Toulouse-Lautrec.

He existed in sparse bohemian quarters along the Left Bank of the Seine River, then one of the poorest, roughest parts of Paris.

It was at this time that he began to do sculptures, even while still producing his gloomy Blue-Period paintings.

Finally, about 1904, Picasso hooked up with some circus people and switched into his brighter, more cheerful Rose-Period style. The paintings, often of clowns and harlequins, also sometimes reflected ancient Greek and Egyptian styles. The "good stuff" lasted only about three years till about 1907, when he set a small part of the art world on its ear with the very first Cubist painting.

What is Cubism, you ask?

Just listen to this definition: "Cubism is the fragmenting of three-dimensional forms into flat areas of pattern and color, overlapping and intertwining so that shapes and parts of the human anatomy are seen from the front and the back at the same time!"

Now, reread that definition and take a look at the real thing, for example, Marcel Duchamp's *Nude Descending a Staircase*. Cubism really caught on throughout Europe and America and it became the dominant style of painting for the first half of the twentieth century. Picasso now turned his hand to trying everything. There was pottery, a series of mistresses, theatre sets, drinking, and becoming a Communist.

One of his most famous paintings, *Guernica*, portrays the horrors (Fascist ones vs. the Communists) during the Spanish Civil War.

QUESTION: After a long and tempestuous life, punctuated by excesses and debaucheries, at what age do you suppose Pablo Picasso died?

ANSWER: He was ninety-one. So guys, grab a paintbrush and your girlfriend, and let's take off for Paris. With any luck, we will make it to age 100!

Ladies' Stockings: Miracle Fabric Arrives in the Nick of Time

Ah yes, silk stockings, one of the vivid memories of my childhood. But this story is primarily not about silk stockings, for ON THIS DAY, October 24, 1939, a new distraction for the male eye became available. Many of my older readers will recall that first day when *nylon* stockings were offered for sale to the American public.

Being an aspiring investigative newsman, I immediately went to several females of "a certain age" and asked them to reveal their memories of the advent of nylon stockings.

"Well, of course, I was only a child, but I do remember my sister being delighted that those baggy, run-prone silk stockings could now be consigned to the ash-can," said one.

"Oh, yes, my boyfriend bought me my first pair of nylons. I can still remember how much I loved their firm feeling and how glad I was not to have to worry about keeping that blasted seam straight!"

Well, I thought, what else might I learn? Next came the sour grapes. "Well, they no sooner had put nylon stockings on the market after promoting them to a fare thee well at the New York World's Fair, when the United States government yanked them off the market to use in the [World War II] war effort, for parachutes, I think," she said.

So on I went in my quest for knowledge. I actually found a lady whose boyfriend was in the 101st Airborne Division during the invasion of Normandy, and she had the antique parachutes to prove it. "He told me that the invention of nylon gave the term 'Hit the Silk' an entirely new meaning," she replied. (It had previously referred to silk bed sheets.)

Nylon—made from coal, water, air, petroleum, agricultural by-products, and natural gas—became the chemical wonder of the age. It had arrived just in the nick of time to replace silk, suddenly cut off by the war with Japan and desperately needed in the war effort.

After World War II, the new miracle fabric was used for many things, including stockings and other kinds of clothing. Nylon was put to work in making everything from tires to toothbrushes.

QUESTION: Would you happen to know which company invented and first marketed nylon in the United States?

ANSWER: E.I. DuPont de Nemours—known familiarly as DuPont—did the job. Founded by a French immigrant, the DuPont Company has been serving the United States since Revolutionary War times, when they produced gunpowder for the troops!

The Erie Canal: Lake Erie and Atlantic Ocean Finally Get Together

I wanted to write about the gunfight at the OK Corral, which also happened ON THIS DAY, but my family wouldn't let me. They insisted that the column should have a more uplifting tone, so here goes.

This is the day when "Clinton's Folly" opened. No, not Bill's, *DeWitt* Clinton's, the mayor of New York City and later governor of New York state. Hmm . . . maybe there *was* a connection! The date was October 26, 1825, when "Clinton's Folly," also known as the Erie Canal, opened for business.

It was *the* engineering marvel of the early eighteenth century, especially notable because at that time, there was not one engineering school in the entire United States. The canal was essentially built with the raw muscle power of horses and humans, coupled with a generous amount of good old Yankee "can-do attitude."

But why were the proponents of the canal so eager to have it built? Well, picture this: after the American Revolution, and until the 1825 opening of the Erie Canal, restless Americans who wished to move westward to make their fortunes were being blocked by the forbidding heights of the Appalachian mountain chain and the almost impassable roads that were rutted, sun-baked mud trails in summer and quagmires of mud, rain, and snow during the winter months. Still, visions of vast timberlands, rich fields of minerals, and fertile farmland kept a trickle of pioneers moving west in spite of the hardships.

By 1816 the pressure to open the West was irresistible. New York City and its mayor, DeWitt Clinton, were understandably all for it. So were the people who lived in western New York state. Even the US Congress easily passed a bill that provided funding for the building of "the marvel of the age." But alas, just when the celebrations had begun, US President James Monroe announced that he thought the idea of the United States funding a New York state canal was unconstitutional! So he promptly vetoed the proposal and New York state was back to square one.

Fortunately, the following year (1817) DeWitt Clinton was elected governor of New York state and he used his many persuasive powers to convince the New York state legislature to authorize funding for a forty-foot-wide, four-foot deep canal running from Buffalo to New York City. The expected cost was more than $7 million and the only promise of repayment came from projected canal tolls, if any, hence the derisive nickname of "Clinton's Folly."

It took eight years to dig, but ON THIS DAY in 1825, Governor Clinton had the pleasure of pouring a cask of Lake Erie water into the Atlantic Ocean at New York City, thus effecting a "marriage of the waters"!

The impact of the canal was immediate and dramatic as eager pioneers headed west, and soon the fruits of their labor were sailing east toward New York City. The Big Apple became the biggest seaport in America with connections to Lake Erie and the vast territories west of Buffalo. Eight percent of upstate New York's population eventually took up residence within twenty-five miles of the Erie Canal.

Despite the coming of the railroad within ten years of the opening of the Erie Canal, the waterway became a huge financial success and Clinton—DeWitt, that is—was a popular hero.

QUESTION: Can you tell me how many miles long that original Erie Canal was?

ANSWER: True to the details of that 1816 survey, the length of "Clinton's ditch" was 363 miles. And it opened ON THIS DAY, October 26, 1825.

The Erie Canal at Pittsford, New York
Credit: Kathryn

NOVEMBER

Even though it doesn't mark the Pilgrims' first landing place, this rock in Plymouth, Massachusetts, is visited by thousands of tourists annually.
Credit: Christian Johnson

The First Thanksgiving: Wise But Wary Pilgrims Say 'Thanks'

The fourth Thursday in November is our Thanksgiving day, as it was finally proclaimed by the Congress of the United States of America in 1941.

But the recorded history of Thanksgiving in America stretches back more than three centuries from that date.

We all know, or think we know, that the Pilgrims celebrated a Thanksgiving meal following the completion of that first arduous year in the New World. It was in the autumn at the time of the fall harvest, so for our convenience, we will just say that it was first enjoyed On This Day in 1621.

The Pilgrims, being wise as well as wary, invited the neighboring Wampanoag Indians over for the feast. They came bearing wild fowl and freshly killed venison. The few available vegetables (Indian corn perhaps) were eaten with the meal, but it was mostly meat-centered and probably didn't even include sweets. So we are pretty sure that the Pilgrim boys and girls weren't gobbling up pies and cakes, nor were they playing with their mashed potatoes while waiting for the nonexistent dessert.

Now, I wasn't there to see the event, but I hear that the festivities of 1621 lasted at least three days, with everyone eating his or her fill and giving thanks for the bounty.

The Pilgrims' table was always set for the benefit of the most important persons there, who got the best and first servings of food. Lesser persons (servants and children) helped cook and serve and then ate the leavings while sitting at the foot of the table.

Food was not passed around. Everyone ate what was nearest. Unlike the Pilgrims, the Indians came and went during the meal, often standing while eating and using only a knife to sever the meat from the bone. At one point, Chief Massasoit even sent some of his braves out to harvest a few more wild fowl to supplement the feast.

The Pilgrims didn't use forks. They ate with spoons, knives, and their fingers and used large cloth napkins for any drippings. Salt would have been on the table but not pepper; however, many spices were used in the cooking process.

No matter what their table manners, I'm sure that it was a joyous occasion. But it was by no means the first Thanksgiving.

Two years earlier, in 1619, other British settlers who were newly arrived at Berkeley Plantation near the Charles River in Virginia knelt and offered "a thanksgiving" for their safe arrival in the New World.

And, of course, for centuries prior to the Pilgrims' arrival, Native Americans celebrated at harvest time with festivals, ceremonial dances, and other expressions of thanks.

QUESTION: Moving forward a bit in our time machine, when do you suppose that Thanksgiving was decreed an official United States holiday? And by whom?

ANSWER: George Washington was the first president to declare Thanksgiving a national holiday (in 1789). That definition lasted until Lincoln issued a Thanksgiving proclamation (in 1863), naming the last Thursday of November to be the day. Next was Franklin D. Roosevelt, who proclaimed it to be the third Thursday in November (in 1939, 1940, and 1941) and finally a joint resolution of the US Congress (in 1941) declared it to be on the fourth Thursday of November forevermore.

Enjoy your wild fowl, venison, and sweetmeats too!

Blackbeard the Pirate
Loses His Head

If you had been alive ON THIS DAY nearly 300 years ago and living along the North Carolina or Virginia coast, you would have undoubtedly been wildly rejoicing at the news that the infamous Blackbeard the pirate had been captured.

Edward Teach (or perhaps his name was Thatch) had been born on some unknown date in Bristol, England, London, England, or somewhere on the island of Jamaica.

It is said that he operated as a privateer for the British, sailing the Caribbean during Queen Anne's War from 1702 to 1713, looting and destroying other ships (mostly French) on behalf of the British. Such are the veils of history; we really don't know.

But we do know that by 1717, Teach was a well-practiced pirate and that he had finally decided to go into business for himself. His business was to terrify other seafaring men, inducing them to turn over their goods, jewels, gold, women, and ships hastily to the fearsome Captain Edward Teach.

Let me tell you, this was one buccaneer who really understood the principles of Marketing 101. He had by this time renamed himself "Blackbeard the Pirate" and had grown a scraggly black beard to cover most of his face. In addition, Teach sported a large mop of unruly black hair, which he sometimes highlighted with long, lighted matches shoved under his hat brim to frame his face with fire as he was going into battle! A big, burly man, Blackbeard further enhanced his menacing appearance with a Royal Navy crimson cape, two swords at his waist, and three braces of pistols and knives in bandoliers across his chest. What a sight he must have been!

Blackbeard fits our imagination's picture of a ferocious, blood-drenched pirate as well as any known free-booter in the history of piracy.

During 1717 and 1718, he absolutely terrorized the ships and coastal plantations along the North Carolina and Virginia coasts. Finally, the planters of that area decided they had had enough. They persuaded the governor of Virginia to send out a Royal Navy ship with orders to take Blackbeard, dead or alive. And they did. In a bloody skirmish near Ocracoke Inlet, off the North Carolina coast, the men of the HMS *Pearl* inflicted twenty-five wounds upon Blackbeard.

QUESTION: Did they finish him off?

ANSWER: Celebrating their victory over the notorious brigand, the Royal Navy sailors cut off his bearded head and sailed back to home base with the bodiless head displayed for all to see on the end of a pole.

It happened ON THIS DAY, November 22, 1718—the end of Edward Teach, known to history as Blackbeard the pirate.

World War I Ends with Versailles Treaty: War No More

Remembering our yearly observance of Veterans Day, it is appropriate to look back to its predecessor, Armistice Day, and to the events immediately following World War I, especially to a crucial vote in the US Senate that was taken ON THIS DAY.

The Great War came to an unofficial end with the signing of an armistice at 11 a.m. on the eleventh day of the eleventh month in 1918. More than nine million soldiers had been killed, millions more wounded, additional millions of civilians left homeless. Both sides were exhausted, and no one wanted to ever see such a catastrophe again.

It took more than a year to officially end World War I with the signing of the Treaty of Versailles, and that period saw political battles every bit as vicious as the military ones that had preceded it.

The Big Three (Great Britain, France, and the United States), after months of in-fighting, finally agreed to the terms upon which peace would officially come to the world.

The trouble was, Great Britain and France did not exactly see eye to eye with US President Wilson's idealistic views of a peace treaty nor, as it turned out, did the Republican-controlled US Senate, which had to ratify the treaty by a two-thirds vote, if it were to involve the United States.

More than ten months before the fighting stopped, Wilson had announced his "Fourteen Points" for ending the war and for establishing a peace treaty. He espoused such niceties as "no secret international agreements, armament reductions, freedom of the seas, the US wants nothing for itself" and most importantly, "the establishment of a League of Nations."

One month after the end of hostilities, Wilson sailed for Europe, making the grand tour of all the Allied capitals and staying on for most of the six-month peace conference, completely ignoring the powerful Republican opposition back home. Wilson compromised away much that he had previously demanded, but succeeded in including the establishment of a League of Nations in the treaty.

The Treaty of Versailles was signed on June 28, 1919, but not by Wilson or any other US representative. The isolationist US Senate refused to approve it ON THIS DAY, November 19, 1919.

QUESTION: How did it all turn out?

ANSWER: The US signed a separate peace treaty with Germany in 1921. President Wilson died of a broken heart. And twenty years later we were again engulfed in a world war that might have been avoided, had the US Senate voted differently ON THIS DAY.

The Seven Years War:
French Nearly Fried by Brits

They say that you can't always tell a book by its cover. For example, the Seven Years War between Great Britain, France, Sweden, Austria, and Prussia lasted for a total of seventy-four years (1689-1763)! Part of that conflict played out in North America and was called the French and Indian War (1754-63), though the major combatants were Great Britain and France aided by their Colonial allies in the New World. The French and Indian War was actually a precursor of the American Revolution fought between Great Britain and the American Colonials and their French allies! What's more, the most important event of the French and Indian War happened On This Day, November 25, 1758, seventeen years before the start of the American Revolution.

Military action in this campaign heated up when the British and Colonial forces went gaily marching, to drum and fife, toward what they thought was a lightly defended French Fort Duquesne, near the site of present-day Pittsburgh. The British had been attempting to capture strategic Fort Duquesne, at the confluence of the Allegheny and Monongahela Rivers, since 1755. So far they had failed. But now the Brits had 6,000 fighting men in the field and they felt they were closer to victory. On September 9, 1758, the British had sent out a decoy force of 800 Regulars and Colonials to attack the fort. These were mostly Highlanders, an elite fighting force steeped in the glory of warfare. The attack was a disaster. More than 300 of the Highlanders were killed. Both of their commanders were among those captured.

But On This Day just three months later, things were different for the French and their Indian allies. The French commander of the fort suddenly realized that their 800 fighting men would be no match for those 6,000 British Regulars, under the command of General John Forbes, who were on their way through the forest to overwhelm Fort Duquesne. The French and Indians wisely evacuated the fort during the night, setting fire to it and its provisions as they left under the cover of darkness.

So it was that ON THIS DAY, November 25, 1758, the main force of the British and American troops marched toward a smoldering and deserted Fort Duquesne. Suddenly they saw an appalling sight! The Indians had decapitated many of the captured Highlanders from the failed raid of September 9 and had impaled their heads on the sharp stakes that formed part of the entrance to the fort! This grisly deed was accompanied by the display of the Highland kilts nailed lower on the posts under their matching heads.

Eventually, the burned French fort was leveled as the British and Americans rebuilt a much larger one. They named it (what else?) Fort Pitt, after the British prime minister who had ordered the campaign to be undertaken. This event is generally recognized as the beginning of the end of French power in North America.

During this conflict, there was a contingent of Colonial Virginians serving in the British Royal American Regiment.

QUESTION: What later famous American military commander was a Lt. Colonel in that regiment?

ANSWER: It was George Washington, who had been fighting for the British cause since 1755, participating in several failed attempts upon the French citadel, which was astride all those strategic waterways controlling the center of the country.

We might also note that, while Washington learned his military niceties serving under the British in the French and Indian War, he also picked up valuable information on how they fought and their command weaknesses that would come in handy during the American Revolution soon to come.

DECEMBER

Photographic proof of the Wright brothers'
first successful airplane flight
Credit: Attributed to Wilbur Wright or Orville Wright

The Wright Brothers:
Next Stop—the Moon

One of the four or five most significant inventions of the twentieth century came to fruition ON THIS DAY, December 17, 1903.

Orville Wright was at the controls when the miracle of breaking the bonds of earth in a powered airplane took place.

Simple as it appeared to be, the miracle didn't just *happen*. Orville and Wilbur had been working on the principles of flight in their spare time for more than seven years before this historic day at Kill Devil Hill near Kitty Hawk, North Carolina. The Wrights were just a couple of bachelor bicycle mechanics from Dayton, Ohio, but boy did they have scientific imaginations!

For three years they had been working with gliders, building and rebuilding them, putting them through wind-tunnel and flight tests, trying out various means of controlling the stability of the aircraft. In addition they had invested much effort in the development and improvement of a powerful, lightweight engine that would be needed to propel the craft.

In the end, it was their revolutionary idea—used to control the direction and stability of the aircraft (they called it "wing warping")—that turned the tide in their favor. And to be honest, luck was with them.

They had been inspired by the early flight experiments of Otto Lilienthal, Octave Chanute, and their many followers. Both of those men had tragically died in crashes of their experimental gliders. But their disciples carried on, and—had they lived—they might just as easily have come up with the same answers as the Wrights did. It was a close race.

Another of their major competitors for the honor of being the "first to fly" was Samuel Pierpont Langley, the Secretary of the Smithsonian Institution. Langley, who had the US government bankrolling his experiments, launched a series of man-carrying powered aerodromes from the decks of a houseboat anchored in the Potomac River. All crashed. His last, failed, attempt came only nine days before the Wrights' success at Kitty Hawk.

Finally the Dayton duo had their great chance, ON THIS DAY, December 17, 1903. There's even a photograph of that amazing leap forward for mankind.

QUESTION: How long did the plane stay in the air, and what distance did it cover on that first powered flight?

ANSWER: Orville piloted the *Wright Flyer* for a total of twelve seconds and covered a distance of 120 feet in that first flight. Of the three additional flights that day, the best effort—with Wilbur at the controls—lasted fifty-nine seconds and touched back down to earth 852 feet from the starting point. Man was on his way to the stars!

Louis Armstrong: Satchmo Blows It

Today is a great day in history—in the history of jazz, anyway—for it was on December 28, 1922, when Louis "Satchmo" Armstrong got that life-changing telegram inviting him to join King Oliver's Creole Jazz Band in Chicago as second trumpet man. The twenty-one-year-old black musician from New Orleans was on his way to Chicago, the new capitol of jazz, and he couldn't have been happier.

Joe "King" Oliver was his idol. The young Louis Armstrong had spent years listening to Oliver play the cornet in New Orleans' Funky Butt Hall. King Oliver had even given Satchmo his first cornet and had taught him the rudiments of playing jazz on it. In fact, King Oliver had been something of a surrogate father to the young New Orleans waif.

Louis Armstrong had a very rough childhood. He was born into a poor, fatherless family around 1901 and spent a great deal of time in correctional institutions. One time he was put away for a whole year for firing a pistol into the air during a New Year's Eve celebration. But he picked up a love of music in wide-open New Orleans from hanging out in dive bars and brothels and marching in funeral processions, absorbing the birth of jazz as a distinctive American art form.

By age sixteen, Satchmo, as he was called, began to play cornet with real jazz bands, learning to read music, to improvise on the horn, and even to write some early jazz licks for the cornet. Finally, his big break came in the form of a job with Kid Ory's Jazz Band, New Orleans' finest.

There were gigs playing on Mississippi River boats, a time in St. Louis, and finally the aforementioned job with King Oliver in Chicago. All of this experience molded the uneducated but talented and determined young man into one of America's best musicians.

QUESTION: We mentioned several times that Louis Armstrong was occasionally known as "Satchmo." Where did that name come from?

ANSWER: "Satchmo" was short for "satchel mouth" in African-American dialect, a reference to that yawning cavity in the middle of his face that was beautifully lined with all those pearly white teeth. Louis "Satchmo" Armstrong took off ON THIS DAY, December 28, 1922, for Chicago and his big chance to become one of the jazz greats.

Louis Armstrong blows his horn at Carnegie Hall in 1947.
Credit: William P. Gottlieb

Beatrix Potter: Potter Hoppy with Peter Rabbit

It is difficult to believe that Beatrix Potter, author and illustrator of Peter Rabbit and his myriad friends, died as recently as ON THIS DAY, December 22, 1943.

Her life was shaped by the attitudes and mores of the Victorian era into which she was born in 1866. Her parents were wealthy and busy, much too busy to personally care for their little girl. Beatrix never went to any public or private school but was left to the supervision of a series of nannies and governesses, as was the norm for children of her social class. Outside playmates were discouraged, and she rarely saw her parents more than once a day. There was of course her brother Bertram, born when she was six, but he was soon shipped off to private school, and then there was no one to play with.

Being a resourceful lass, Beatrix Potter invented her own companions, "delighting" Nanny with a menagerie of pets that she studied, played with, drew surprisingly good pictures of, and finally made up stories about. At one time the nursery housed a green frog, a pet hedgehog, a spaniel dog, two lizards, some water newts, a dormouse, a ring-snake, a black Berkshire pig, a tortoise, and of course a succession of rabbits.

As Beatrix grew older, she became a skilled writer, recording for her own pleasure the adventures of many of her animal friends. She kept all of her writings, including a personal diary, in a secret code, to shelter it from prying eyes!

Life proceeded at a slow pace in Victorian England, especially for one so shielded from outside human contact. So it was not until Beatrix Potter was fully grown, at age twenty-seven, to be exact, that she tried to have published

The Tale of Peter Rabbit, a story she had first written and illustrated in a letter to a sick five-year-old boy.

Publishers were unanimous in their opinion of *Peter Rabbit*—they hated it. And so seven more years would pass until she finally decided to have it printed using her own resources. And then it took off, becoming one of the most famous stories ever written.

Through her writings, Miss Potter became quite financially well off. She finally married at age forty-seven, against her elderly parents' wishes, and lived happily ever after, setting up The National Trust to preserve land, buildings, and history in England.

When she died ON THIS DAY in 1943 at age seventy-seven, Beatrix Potter willed 4,000 acres to The National Trust, thus preserving the ecological beauty of her beloved English Lake District.

QUESTION: How many Potter-inspired storybook characters can you name?

ANSWER: Well, among others, there were Peter Rabbit, Squirrel Nutkin, Jemima Puddleduck, Flopsy, Mopsy, and Cottontail, Benjamin Bunny, Mr. Tod, Mrs. Tiggy-Winkle, and a sleepy little dormouse named Xarifa. Sound familiar?

Carry Nation: Hatchet Woman Cuts a Wide Swath

It was a smashing success, one might say, for it was ON THIS DAY, December 27, 1901, that Carry Nation began the violent phase of her career as a prohibitionist by breaking up barrooms with a big hatchet! She was a formidable-looking figure, six feet tall, 180 pounds, clad from head to toe in black, sometimes even wearing a heavy black veil!

Carry had been born in Kentucky in 1846 and had moved with her family to Missouri when she was nine. At age nineteen, an arranged marriage paired her with Dr. Charles Gloyd, a severe alcoholic who promptly fathered a daughter and then drank himself to death within two years of their marriage.

For eight miserable years, Carry nourished her hatred of "demon rum" as she tried valiantly to perform the dual roles of single mom and rural schoolteacher. Finally in 1877, ON THIS DAY, as a matter of fact, Carry married Dr. David A. Nation, an attorney, minister, and newspaper editor who was some nineteen years her senior.

During most of her marriage to Dr. Nation, Carry indulged herself in peacefully organizing, lecturing, and protesting against the sale of alcoholic beverages. When this didn't bring about the desired results, she and her hymn-singing, Bible-carrying, hatchet-toting female cohort laid plans for actually raiding barrooms and breaking up bottles and equipment while holding barroom prayer sessions.

That brings us to her activities ON THIS DAY, December 27, 1901, the final day of the Women's Christian Temperance Union convention in Topeka, Kansas. This was the day when Carry Nation's prohibitionist ladies stalked the streets of that city in an effort to close up or break up all of Topeka's illegal liquor establishments. Her activities had the desired effect.

For the next nine years, Carry was regularly arrested and jailed for her intemperate temperance activities. She eventually hit the lecture circuit, using the entrance fees to pay all of her fines. Carry Nation even became a European celebrity when she made a yearlong temperance tour of the Continent during 1908-09.

QUESTION: How do you suppose the story of this unholy temperance terror ends?

ANSWER: Well, let's see. Her second husband divorced her, she declared herself to be divinely inspired to continue applying the hatchet to offending saloons, and she finally died at age sixty-five, in 1911 and was buried in an obscure grave in Belton, Missouri. Her grave is now marked by a monument erected in her honor by the Women's Christian Temperance Union. And to think it all began ON THIS DAY, December 27, 1901. What more is there to say? Cheers!

Credit: NASA

Crew of Apollo 8 Reads the Gospel: Luke Speaks from Space

December 24: everyone knows what happened ON THIS DAY (or on the next day or *sometime* during the reign of Caesar Augustus).

The actual date is not so important as the actual event, one that divided the millennia into BC and AD and changed the world forever.

But *this* December 24th occurred in 1968 when things were going badly, at least for the United States of America. Some already knew that the war in Vietnam was lost; others would soon be apprised of that fact.

However, in the area of space travel, things were looking up—literally! The United States was on its way to the moon. We were not quite ready for a moon landing, but on Christmas Eve 1968, Apollo 8 was already in orbit around the lunar surface. And ON THIS DAY an amazing thing happened.

The whole world seemed to stop, as it turned its collective attention skyward . . . to listen, to think, and to be inspired by three young American military officers speaking these familiar words from the Gospel of Luke: "And she brought forth her firstborn son, and wrapped him in swaddling clothes, and laid him in a manger because there was no room for them in the inn . . . And the angel said unto the shepherds, 'Fear not: for, behold, I bring you good tidings of great joy, which shall be to all people . . . Glory to God in the highest and on earth peace, good will toward all men.'"

I hope that you, too, may be inspired by the beauty and meaning of these words on Christmas Eve, even decades after they were broadcast from Apollo 8 as it circled the heavenly body.

QUESTION: Because we always end by asking you to search your memories, who were those *Bible*-reading Apollo 8 astronauts?

ANSWER: Frank Borman, James Lovell, and William Anders inspired us from the heavens ON THIS DAY, December 24, 1968.

Edwards Brothers Malloy
Thorofare, NJ USA
April 23, 2015